Mail Art by Sending Stones: A Reader
Michio Horikawa + Reiko Tomii

石を送るメール・アート読本

堀川紀夫＋富井玲子

目次

—

本書の構成

—

本書の準備は、堀川紀夫の《石を送るメール・アート》シリーズにまつわる作品集として出発した。その制作過程で、作家の執筆する「覚書」が、当時の作家の考えや数々の郵送や取材に関するエピソードなどを取り込んで、詳細な自筆年譜の様相を呈するようになった。これは、作家の多弁な文章作法によるところも少なくないが、むしろ《石を送るメール・アート》が単なるモノとしての作品に閉じることなく、《石》を通じて、また《石》から派生してくる言葉を通じて、人と人を繋げるネットワークの生成装置のような役割を果たしていることに負うところが多いのではないか、との結論に至った。つまり《石を送るメール・アート》は、オープンに開かれた作品であり、本書に再録・掲載されたアメリカ人批評家二人による評論や日本人美術史家による三本の論考も、《石》の紡ぎだしたネットワークの一部なのである。

　この理解に基づき、本書は「読本」として出版される。つまり、通常の作品集のように作品を見るのみではなく、作品を契機として出現した思索や観察や意見をも読むための本となった。（富井玲子）

Contents

–

About This Book

–

We began this book project centering on Horikawa Michio's *Mail Art by Sending Stones* with a conventional monograph in mind. However, as the artist articulated his thoughts on the series and narrated a number of episodes surrounding his mailings and interviews he gave newspaper reporters, a simple "Notes" grew into a full-fledged "Chronicle." The expansion was as much due to his prolific writing style as informed by the fact that *Stones* is not a self-contained work, but functioned as a mechanism generating words on *Stones* that link those involved into an expansive network. In other words, *Stones* is an open work. Together with the artist's chronicle, two exhibition reviews by two American art critics and three essays by a Japanese art historian included in this volume constitute a part of this vast network resulting from *Stones*.

Based on this understanding, this volume is presented as "a reader," that requires not only "looking at" the work but also "reading" the thoughts, observations, and opinions deriving from the work. (RT)

本書全体

–

1　美術作品の題名は《　》で表記する。

2　出版物については書籍題名、記事題名をそれぞれ『　』、「　」で表記する。

3　展覧会題名については「　」、あるいは鉤括弧なし（覚書のみ）で表記した。

4　文中《石》とあるのは、《石を送るメール・アート》のシリーズ題名の略称であり、郵送した個々の石の略称でもある。

覚書

–

5　年月日を見出しとする年譜形式で事項を記述した。

6　年月日の表記は以下のとおり。

　　　　1971.1 = 1971 年 1 月

　　　　1971.1.1 = 1971 年 1 月 1 日

　　　　1971 夏 = 1971 年夏

　　　　1971.1 頃 = 1971 年 1 月頃

7　《石を送るメール・アート》の個別作品のデータを以下のように構成する。

　　　　タイトル

　　　　送付数

　　　　送付先

　　　　テキスト記述

8　《石を送るメール・アート》の個別作品のタイトルについては、英語表記を原則とする。

9　書誌や展覧会題名については、読みやすさを優先させて、一部の例外を除いて和訳した。[E]（＝英語）を付した書誌、および国外の人名や展覧会名の原語データについては、英文テキスト「A Chronicle」を参照されたい。

Legends

–

1　East Asian names are rendered in the traditional manner, surname first. Exceptions are made to those who reside outside Japan and adopt the Western order (e.g., On Kawara; Shūsaku Arakawa).

2　In transliterating the Japanese language, the modified Hepburn Romanization system has been employed. A notable deviation from the original Hepburn is the use of "n" before b, m, and p (e.g., shinbun, Anpo).

3　Macrons are used to indicate long vowels in Japanese names and words (e.g., Takiguchi Shūzō). Commonly known place names and words adopted into English are given without macrons (e.g., Tokyo).

4　In texts, where *Stone* or *Stones* are used, they refer to either the series *Mail Art by Sending Stones* or the individual stone[s] sent in the series.

5　In "A Chronicle," the following conventions are adopted.

5.1　Entries are chronologically organized with the date as an entry heading.

5.2　Dates are given in an abridged manner:

　　　　1971.1 = January 1971

　　　　1971.1.1 = January 1, 1971

　　　　1971 summer = Summer of 1971

5.3　Data of each *Stone* mailing are organized as follows:

　　　　Title

　　　　Number of stones sent

　　　　Addressees

5.4　Where necessary, the data are followed by annotations.

5.5　For the sake of readability, all the exhibition and publication titles in Japanese are presented in English translation. Japanese titles thus presented are indicated by [J] at the end.

はじめに
—

《石を送るメール・アート》（以下《石》）は前衛表現を目指す「新潟現代美術家集団GUN」の旗印のもと、十日町市中条の信濃川で1969.7.21のアポロ11号人類史上初の月面探査、「月の石」採取に因む宇宙時に「地球の石」を採取して始まりました。

時はベトナム戦争の最中。採取された石を針金で結え、荷札に宛名を書いて切手を貼り、メール・アートに仕立て、「月の石より地球の石を考えよう」「月のことより地球の現実を考えよう」という大きなメッセージを込めて作家や評論家に送りました。それが予想を超えた高い視点から批評、コメントされ美術雑誌、新聞に取り上げられ、翌年の中原佑介コミッショナーによる国際的な発表の場、第10回東京ビエンナーレ——人間と物質展に招待される機会に恵まれました。

その後、生業の中学校の美術教師の傍らで作家として《石》の成果を発展させる野心を描き、71年に《石》に不可欠なアイテムである切手の型を借用して《零円切手》を考案。それで時の総理大臣を風刺。それは以後の表現展開の原型の一つになりましたが、《石》の上を行く作品にはなり得ませんでした。72年の17号でアポロ計画が終了し、「因む」という《石》の根拠が失われ、以後《石》を断念。自分が成してきた《石》のメタ言語が見えていませんでした。それは私の浅学と経験不足によるものでした。

自他ともに納得のいくような表現を求めて試行錯誤を重ね75年に無意識的に身体を使うボディ・アートに越境し身体が表現生成の原点であることを改めて認識。

76年に《零円切手》路線で個展をした際には、風刺が原因で週刊誌で掲載拒否になって無念の思いがありました。気を取り直し、あぶり出し絵画や地元産の石を彫るなどの試みの後、80年代に入って新雪に五体投地した跡を写し撮るボディ・アート《Snow Performance》を発見。おおよそ10年の表現探査の末に作家としてのメタ・アートの力を身につけることができたと思いました。しばらくの間《Snow Performance》を展開し続け80年代末に、アクリル絵具を用いた表現で新境地に辿り着きましたが、96年1月にはNHK人間マップ「先生は雪のアーチスト」に《Snow Performance》で出演。その際に《石》も放映される機会に恵まれました。その翌年には、彦坂尚嘉による『アクリラート』32号でのロングインタビューでGUNと自らの歩みが総括され、《石》の再評価を得るなどで、その後への確かな展望を持つことができました。そして、その記事がNYを拠点に活躍している美術史家の富井玲子の目に止まり、《石》が2001年のTate Modernが企画したセンチュリー・シティ展東京セクションに招待されました。その機会に《石》に込めた意味が全く色褪せてはいないことに改めて思いを馳せ、その再開に踏み切りました。

08年に前山忠と『新潟現代美術家集団GUNの軌跡』を出版。12年には新潟県立近代美術館で、GUN——新潟に前衛があった頃展が開催され《石》とその関係資料を網羅した展示がありました。16年には富井が英文著作『荒野のラジカリズム』でGUNの《雪のイメージを変えるイベント》や《石》を世界に発信。18年のMisa Shin Gallery個展では、Not a Stone's Throw（石を投げるほどには近くはない）展で《石》に新しい意味が付加され、19年には荒野のラジカリズム：グローバル60年代の日本の美術家たち展でNYデビュー。20年にはコロナ禍を受けてオンライン雑誌『4Columns.com』に登場と《石》が脚光を浴びることが続いてきています。一つの《石》の表現が、「たかが地球の石されど地球の石」で50年以上存命してきました。

これまでの《石》の生成から50年以上の経緯を振り返り、富井と二人三脚の作品集の出版を思い立ちました。《石》の「覚書」には多数の皆様よりいただいた批評とコメント、および自写のものと新聞社から撮影していただいた写真を時系列にまとめました。作家論は、2000年以降に執筆された富井論文2編に新たな書き下ろし1編、またアメリカ人批評家による展評2編を加えさせていただきました。和訳英訳ともに翻訳はすべてが富井によるものです。

堀川紀夫

Foreword

—

Mail Art by Sending Stones (hereafter *Stones*) was launched on the dry riverbed of the Shinano River in the Nakajō area of Tōkamachi in Niigata Prefecture under the banner of GUN: Niigata Contemporary Artists Collective, on July 21, 1969. I gathered "earth stones" there, in conjunction with the gathering of "moon rocks" conducted during the Apollo 11 mission, which accomplished the first lunar landing by humankind.

It was in the midst of the Vietnam War. I wound wires around the stones I had gathered and attached stamped and addressed mail tags to eleven stones. I sent this mail-art work to artists and critics with expansive messages, "Let us think more of earth stones than moon rocks" and "Let us think more of the reality on the earth than the moon." These and subsequent *Stones* went on to receive critical comments and attention from an unexpectedly lofty perspective in newspapers and art magazines. In the following year, I was given a great opportunity by Nakahara Yūsuke, the commissioner of *Tokyo Biennale 1970: Between Man and Matter*, to show my *Stones* in this exhibition.

From then onward, I envisioned an ambitious project of expanding my *Stones* as an artist, while working as a middle-school art teacher to make a living. In 1971, I devised a series of *Zero-Yen Stamps*, focusing on the stamp, an indispensable element of *Stones*, to satirize the prime minister at the time. This became a foundation for one of my continuing explorations, but *Stamps* never surpassed *Stones*. In 1972, when the Apollo program ended with the Apollo 17 mission, I lost the principle of "in conjunction" that underscored my *Stones* series and I decided to conclude it, for at the time I could not see a meta language latent in *Stones*, due to my inexperience and ignorance.

By 1975, through trial and error, my search for an expression compelling to the eye of both myself and others led me to body art: as I deployed my body in an unconscious state, I reconfirmed the fact that my body is the starting point of expression.

In 1976, I had a solo exhibition featuring the *Zero-Yen Stamps* series. At that time, I felt utterly disappointed by the rejection by a weekly magazine to illustrate my *Stamps*. As I resumed my search, I tried to carve stones (of local origins) and paint with invisible ink (images that would reveal themselves with application of heat). Entering the 1980s, I discovered *Snow Performance* as a type of body art, in which I threw my body onto newly accumulated snow and photographed the imprint.

I continued *Snow Performance* for a while, and by the late 1980s, I arrived at a new expression in acrylic painting. In January 1996, I appeared in an episode of "Teacher Is a Snow Artist" in NHK's television series "Human Map." My *Stones* were also included in the episode. In the following year, the artist Hikosaka Naoyoshi conducted and published a long interview with me in *Acrylart*, no. 32. This not only gave me an opportunity to look back on the activities of GUN and myself, but also led to a renewed interest in *Stones*, a development that was very encouraging to me. Reiko Tomii, a New York–based art historian, saw this interview and decided to include my *Stones* in the Tokyo section of *Century City*, an exhibition at Tate Modern in 2001. On this occasion, I came to realize that the idea I imbued *Stones* with was still relevant and decided to resume the series.

In 2008, Maeyama Tadashi and I co-published *Trajectory of GUN: Niigata Contemporary Artists Collective*, which was followed in 2012 by *GUN: Niigata Contemporary Artists Group and Its Era*, a retrospective exhibition at Niigata Prefectural Museum of Modern Art, where *Stones* and related documents were exhibited. In 2016, Tomii published *Radicalism in the Wilderness: International Contemporaneity and 1960s Art in Japan*, which presented GUN's *Event to Change the Image of Snow* and my *Stones* series to the whole world. Two years later, in 2018, my solo exhibition *Not a Stone's Throw* at Misa Shin Gallery in Tokyo expanded the horizon of its relevance. And finally, in 2019, my work made an exhibition debut in New York with *Radicalism in the Wilderness: Japanese Artists in the Global 1960s*. This led in 2020 to an online essay on *Stones* on *4Columns.com*. *Stones* has thus continued to receive a series of recognitions. "Just a stone yet a stone," the mail-art series has survived more than 50 years.

In compiling this book, I wanted to chronicle the 50-plus years of *Stones* from the beginning in collaboration with Tomii. "A Chronicle" consists of chronological data as well as critical texts and comments given to *Stones*, illustrated by photographs I myself shot and those taken by newspaper companies. Tomii contributed three texts, two previously published and one newly written for this volume. Two reviews by two American art critics are also reprinted. All translations, English to/from Japanese, are done by Tomii.

Horikawa Michio

Mail Art by Sending Stones: A Chronicle
Horikawa Michio

《石を送るメール・アート》覚書

堀川紀夫

1969.7.21

生徒と信濃川の河原に出かけて「地球の石」採取した。写りは良くないがネガに残る一番最初の画像である

= Together with my students, I go to a dry riverbed of the Shinano River and gather "earth stones." Though a little blurry, they are the first images preserved in the form of negatives.

1964

新潟大学教育学部高田分校中学校美術科入学。入学ひと月後の5月にルーブル美術館からミロのビーナスが来日したのを見に初めて東京へ旅行した。東京へは行きも帰りも夜行列車で片道6時間くらいの長旅だった。会場の西洋美術館へ入館するまで行列が科学博物館を左回りに1周した。その後、近くの東京都美術館で毎日新聞社主催の現代日本美術展を見た。オリンピックをテーマにした特別展示があり記憶に残っている。これ以後、年2回以上は東京へ展覧会、画廊巡りに行くようになった。

1965

長岡現代美術館の存在を知り、常設展、長岡現代美術館賞展を見始める。

1967.8

長岡現代美術館で現代アメリカ絵画展を見る。ウォーホルの《16のジャッキーの肖像》、ローゼンクイストの《成長計画》などが強く印象に残る。

1967.10

1年先輩の前山忠のリードのもと新潟現代美術家集団GUNの結成に加わり、現代美術の活動を目指し始める。

『美術ジャーナル』61号の「作家の記録　虚空間状況探知センター　松沢宥」を読む。

1967.12

新潟現代美術家集団GUN展（ギャラリー新宿、東京）に参加。会場にて写真家、羽永光利と出会う。以後上京の折に泊めていただくことになる。

1968.3

大学卒業に当たり親からダブルのスーツをオーダーメイドしてもらった。そのスーツが新作のヒントとなった。洋服屋が縫製に使った型紙を転用しキャンバス地の上着を発注制作した。それが自分にとって最初の発注アートだった。その発想のヒントはオルデンバークの作品だった。

1964

I enroll in the middle-school art teachers' section at the Takada branch of Niigata University in April. In May, I travel for the first time to Tokyo, to see the *Venus de Milo* on loan from the Louvre at the National Museum of Western Art. I use the night train both ways, each trip taking as long as six hours. There is a long line to enter the museum that passes the neighboring National Museum of Nature and Science and goes around a full park block. At the nearby Tokyo Metropolitan Art Museum, I see the *6th Contemporary Art Exhibition of Japan*, organized by the Mainichi newspaper company. Of particular interest is an Olympic-themed special display. Thereafter, I will go to Tokyo to make the rounds of galleries and see exhibitions more than twice a year.

1965

I become aware of the existence of Museum of Contemporary Art, Nagaoka (opened in 1964). I begin to visit it to see its collection displays and the Nagaoka Contemporary's Award Exhibition.

1967.8

I see an exhibition of contemporary American paintings at the Nagaoka Contemporary. I am particularly impressed by Warhol's *Sixteen Jackies* and Rosenquist's *Growth Plan*.

1967.10

I join in the founding of GUN: Niigata Contemporary Artists Collective under the leadership of Maeyama Tadashi, one year my senior at the university, and begin to explore contemporary art activities.

I read "Artist's Document: Void/Imaginary Space Situation Research Center—Matsuzawa Yutaka" in *Bijutsu Journal*, no. 61.

1967.12

I participate in the exhibition of GUN: Niigata Contemporary Artists Collective at Gallery Shinjuku in Tokyo. I become acquainted with the photographer Hanaga Mitsutoshi at the exhibition. Hereafter, he will put me up at his home when I go to Tokyo.

1968.3

My parents have a double-breasted suit made to order for me upon my graduation. The suit led me to make a new work: I order a canvas jacket based on the paper patterns that a tailor used for my suit. It is my first

1968.4
十日町市立中条中学校に教員採用される。

学校近くの屋根板金屋の倉庫2階に下宿。部屋の下には素材としての沢山のトタン板と鏡面ステンレスが積まれていた。その鏡面ステンレスを用いてネクタイのオブジェ《収束》を制作する。

1968.8
新潟現代美術家集団GUN展（長岡文化会館ホール）に参加。関根伸夫、田中信太郎、小島信明、野中ユリが特別出品として招待された。外界を写し込む拙作のステンレス作品の《収束》に、関根伸夫から「ファッションが変わるかも」というコメントがあった。

1968.10
GUN展で知己を得た関根伸夫が《位相－大地》で受賞した話が伝わってきて驚かされる。

1968.11
十日町市展にフレームの立方体とその対角線にゴム紐を張って蛍光塗料を塗った《Space》を出品。また、地元の朔風会のメンバーとのグループ展で画廊に蛍光塗料を塗ったゴム紐による角柱を張り巡らし、ブラックライトで照らす作品を出品。

1969.1
『美術手帖』で「世界の動向：自然を造形する　アメリカのあたらしい動き・観念の芸術としての「アースワーク」」（美術記者・泉治郎）（20–21頁）を見る。

『デザイン批評』掲載のアラン・ジュフロワ「芸術の廃棄」（峯村敏明訳）を読む。

1969.4
『美術手帖』で石子順造の記事「今月の焦点：高松次郎個展の問題提起」（12–13頁）を見る。この記事で図版掲載されていた石を使った作品《シリーズNo.7》の写真を見て、勤務校のすぐ近くに流れる信濃川の広大な河原の無尽蔵の石に目が向く。

fabricated work (*hatchū geijutsu*). The inspiration comes from Oldenburg's work.

1968.4
I am appointed an art teacher at Tōkamachi City Naka-jō Middle School.

I find a room on the second floor of a storehouse owned by a purveyor of sheet-metal roofs near my school. I see piles of galvanized iron sheets for roofing and mirrored stainless-steel sheets on the storehouse's first floor. I make a necktie-shaped sculpture, *Convergence*, with the mirrored stainless steel.

1968.8
I participate in the exhibition of GUN: Niigata Contemporary Artists Collective at Nagaoka Culture Hall. We invite Sekine Nobuo, Tanaka Shintarō, Kojima Nobuaki, and Nonaka Yuri to show their works as special guests. Sekine Nobuo comments on my *Convergence*, which reflects the external world, saying "It may change the fashion."

1968.10
I am surprised to learn that Sekine Nobuo, whose acquaintance I gained through GUN's exhibition, wins an award with his *Phase—Mother Earth* at *Kobe Suma Rikyū Park Contemporary Art Exhibition*.

1968.11
I show *Space*, a skeletal cube with rubber strings diagonally stretched and painted in day-glo colors, at Tōkamachi City Exhibition. I also show another work with day-glo-painted rubber strings, which I stretch on a square column and light by black light at a group exhibition with members of the local group Sakufū-kai.

1969.1
I see a mention of Earthworks in "World Trends: Making Art from Nature: A New American Movement, Earthworks as Art of Concept" (by art reporter Izumi Jirō) in *Bijutsu techō* (pp. 20–21).

I read Alain Geoffroy's "Abandonment of Art" (Geijutsu no haiki), translated by Minemura Toshiaki, in the magazine *Dezain hihyō/The Design Review*.

1969.4
I see Ishiko Junzō's r eport, "Focus of This Month: An Issue Raised by Takamatsu Jirō's Solo Exhibition" in

1969.4.2

前山に同行して石子順造のアパートを訪問した際に、静岡・幻触グループの丹羽勝次が直方体の郵便物を投射図的に平面に造形したトリック表現の《箱》のメール・アートと高松次郎の《点》シリーズの針金オブジェを見る機会を得る。長野県下諏訪町在住の作家松澤宥の葉書で送る郵送アートなどについて教示を受けた。

この頃より、ユニーク作品の発想を目指して思い付きのメモを心がけるようになる。

1969.5

第9回現代日本美術展の平面と立体のコンクール部門に応募するも落選。

第9回現代日本美術展を見る。飯田昭二《トランスマイグレーション》、河原温《Pictorial Diary》、小池一誠《石》、関根伸夫《空相（水）》などが印象に残る。

箱根の森美術館で開催される第1回国際彫刻展の公募部門を目指して、いくつかの野外作品を構想するも応募には至らなかった。

1969.7

『美術手帖』で「特集：新しい自然＝エレメンタリズム〈2〉アースワーク」を見る。高松次郎が多摩川中流で《石と数字》を制作している写真が信濃川と重なって見えた。

1969.7.1

朝、腹部に激しい疼痛を感じる。尿管結石になって病気休暇、一時入院など。休みを取って実家に帰って、中央病院で投薬を受けるなど療養する。

1969.7.14

職場へ復帰

1969.7.15

学校で生徒とアポロ8号、9号の記録映画の巡回放映を見る。

Bijutsu techō (pp. 12–13). Seeing a photo of stone-based *Series No. 7* accompanying the text, I think of countless stones on a vast dry riverbed along the Shinano River near my school.

1969.4.2

I accompany Maeyama Tadashi, a fellow member of GUN, to Tokyo and visit the critic Ishiko Junzō at his apartment, where I see *Point*, one of Takamatsu Jirō's *objet* series, and Niwa Katsuji's *Mail Art by Box*, that looks like a packaged box depicted in a distorted perspective. I learn about Matsuzawa Yutaka's mail art for which he sent postcards from Shimo Suwa in central Japan, where he lives.

From around this time, I make it a habit to keep notes of ideas in order to train myself to create original works.

1969.5

My submission to the competitive sections for two- and three-dimensional works at *9th Contemporary Art Exhibition of Japan* is rejected.

I see *9th Contemporary Art Exhibition of Japan* at Tokyo Metropolitan Art Museum. I am impressed by Iida Shōji's *Transmigration*, On Kawara's *Pictorial Diary* (part of his *I Got Up* postcard series), Koike Kazushige's *Stone*, and Sekine Nobuo's *Phase—Water*.

I plan in vain a few outdoor works for the competitive section of the inaugural *Contemporary International Sculpture* held by Hakone Open-Air Museum.

1969.7

I see "Special Feature: New Nature (2)—Elementalism 'Earthworks'" in *Bijutsu techō*. A photo of Takamatsu Jirō making *Stone and Numeral* at the middle section of the Tama River reminds me of the Shinano River.

1969.7.1

In the morning, I feel an acute pain in my stomach. It turns out I suffer from a urinary calculus. I take sick leave during temporary hospitalization. I go back to my parents' house to rest, while receiving medicine at the Central Hospital.

1969.7.14

I return to work.

1969.7 中旬
関根伸夫の《空相（石）》が箱根彫刻の森美術館の現代国際彫刻展で受賞した話が伝わってくる。

瀧口修造『マルセル・デュシャン語録』（美術出版社）を 1968.12 に購入。その荒川修作のオマージュ図版の TITLE.NAME.DATE を記載するフレームに倣ってデータカードを印刷し、メール・アートの記録の整理などに使用した。

1969.7.17–25
アポロ 11 号 打ち上げ、月面着陸、船外活動、地球帰還

1969.7.17
米国フロリダ州ケネディ宇宙センターよりアポロ 11 号が打ち上げられる。人類史上初めて月面に着陸して石を拾って帰ってくるという。そんなニュースが駆け巡る中で、このタイミングに合わせて地球で石を拾ってメール・アートとして送れば話題になるのではと考えた。東北地方にあるというこけしを郵送する方法を援用して、アポロ 11 号が月の石を拾うことに合わせて、地球で石を拾い「石を針金で梱包して郵送する」ことを思い付く。その時の気持ちは地球上でこのような発想をした人は他にもいるかもしれない。とにかくやってみよう。「やらなかったことで後悔はしたくはない」ということであった。しかし決行するかどうかは 2 日間くらい逡巡した。

1969.7.21
The Shinano River Plan: 11
送付数：11
送付先
　石子順造
　郭仁植
　関根伸夫
　高松次郎*
　東野芳明
　中原佑介
　針生一郎
　前田常作
　松沢宥

1969.7.15
At school, together with my students, I watch a traveling documentary film program about the Apollo 8 and 9 missions.

1969.7 (midmonth)
I learn that Sekine Nobuo's *Phase of Nothingness—Stone* received an award at the inaugural *Contemporary International Sculpture* at Hakone Open-Air Museum.

Around this time, I have data cards printed. They are modeled after Shūsaku Arakawa's "diagram painting" which bears a data box for title, name, and date. The work was included in the deluxe edition of the Japanese translation of *To and from Rrose Selavy: Selected Words of Marcel Duchamp* by Takiguchi Shūzō, which I acquired in December 1968. I use these data cards to organize the records of mail art.

1969.7.17–25
The Apollo 11 mission encompasses its launch, lunar landing, extravehicular activities on the lunar surface, and flight home.

1969.7.17
Apollo 11 is launched from Kennedy Space Center in Florida. I learn that the mission involves a lunar landing and gathering of moon rocks, the first in human history. As the news goes around, I think of making my own news by collecting earth stones and sending them as mail art in conjunction with this landmark event. I decide to collect earth stones simultaneously with the Apollo 11 crew's moon rock gathering, and "bind my stones with wires" for postal mailing similar to the "*kokeshi*-doll mail" in the Tōhoku region. My thought is: even if there is another person who might have the exact same idea, I will just do it; if I didn   t, I would regret it forever. However, I remain undecided for two days before I finally decide to do it.

1969.7.21
The Shinano River Plan: 11
Number of stones sent: 11
Addressees
　Ishiko Junzō
　Kwak In-Sik
　Sekine Nobuo
　Takamatsu Jirō*
　Tōno Yoshiaki

前山忠（GUN のメンバー）
本人

* 名前の下線は、それまでに直接会ったことのない人物を意味する。以下同様。

アポロ 11 号月面着陸の当日、朝からアポロ 11 号が月に到着したとラジオとテレビで実況中継番組が放送されていた。その日は良い天気だった、前日に決行を決めて準備はしていた。月探査船が月に着陸したのは朝 5 時過ぎで（日本時間、以下同様）、一部始終がラジオで中継放送されていた。アームストロング船長が船外に出て、人類が月面に記念すべき一歩を記したのは 11 時 56 分 20 秒だった。

その中継放送をトランジスタラジオで流しながら、3 限の 1 年 C 組の美術授業として校外学習の名目で学校近くの信濃川に出かけ、生徒と共に石を採取した。

生徒には、人類が月面に到着して月の石を拾うので、その宇宙の同時間にこの信濃川で「地球の石を拾う」という体験的学習の意味を伝えた。

信濃川は、学校から 300 メートルほどのところにある。石は無尽蔵にあるので、それを拾うという課題だけでは数分でできてしまう。だから台秤を持って行き、300g の重さを目指せと指示した。生徒は計りで確かめながら石を拾ってくれた（Fig. 1.1）。

石はアポロ 11 号に合わせ 11 個以上は拾った。バケツに入れて持ち帰った。それぞれの石について厳密にデータを取ったわけではない。放課後になったのでメール・アートに仕立てる荷造りを急いだ（Fig. 1.2）。

石と荷札に月着陸船が月面に 4 本の足を下ろした時刻 517420 * とアームストロング船長が月に足跡を記した瞬間の 115620 と日付 44.7.21 と名前 GUN Horikawa Michio をスタンプした。郵送する前に《石を送るメール・アート》の荷姿を数枚撮影し、最寄りの魚沼中条郵便局へ持ち込み、自分を含めた 11 人の作家と美術評論家に送った。（*新聞報道には 5 時 17 分 40 秒と記載されていた。）

その郵送を果たした時、《石》の成功を確信していたわけではなかった。《石》の未来は全く見えていなかった。

《石》の郵送後に、友人つき合いしていた教え子の高校 1 年生と河原に出かけその日 2 度目の「石拾い」を行った。

河原での 2 回の石拾いのプロセスの一部は、当時の

Nakahara Yūsuke
Haryū Ichirō
Maeda Jōsaku
Matsuzawa Yutaka
Maeyama Tadashi (GUN member)
Myself

* Underlined names indicate those I have not personally met before.

On the day of Apollo 11's lunar landing, the news is broadcast live on radio and television from the morning. It is a fine day. The day before, I decided to undertake my stone gathering and got ready. At five a.m. (all times are local time in Japan), the lunar module lands on the moon, with the whole proceedings being aired on radio. Commander Neil Armstrong disembarks and marks the memorable first step on the moon surface at 11:56:20.

During the third-period art class, I take the seventh graders of C Class out to the Shinano River under the pretext of field study. I bring a transistor radio with me so that we can listen to the live broadcast of the lunar surface activities. While listening to the radio, I gather stones with my students. I tell them that it will be an important occasion of hands-on learning when they "gather earth stones" along the Shinano River at the very same cosmic time when humans land on the moon and gather moon rocks there.

The Shinano River is located about 300 meters from our school. We bring a kitchen scale so that we can weigh our stones. There are countless stones on the dry riverbed, so it would take only a short time to complete our mission if we set no parameters. So I tell them to pick stones each weighing around 300 grams. They carefully weigh their stones to ensure their stones fit our parameter (Fig. 1.1).

In conjunction with the mission number, we gather more than 11 stones just in case. I then bring them to school in a bucket. I take no data of these stones. After school, I hastily prepare the 11 stones for mailing (Fig. 1.2).

On the *Stones* themselves and mail tags, I stamp my name (GUN Horikawa Michio), the Japanese time of the landing (517420*), and the date and time of Armstrong's stepping on the moon (44**.7.21, 115620). [*Newspaper reports give 5:17:40, **11 means Shōwa 11 in the Japanese era, equivalent to 1969.] I take a few photos of the prepared *Stones* for the project to be known as *Mail Art by Sending Stones*. I then head to the nearby Uonuma Nakajō Post Office. I send 11 stones to 11 people, that

Fig. 1.1　　*The Shinano River Plan: 11*, 1969
　　　　　　秤で石の重さを確認する生徒たち = Students weighing stones with a kitchen scale

Fig. 1.2　　*The Shinano River Plan: 11*, 1969
　　　　　　メール・アートに仕立てた石 11 個 = 11 stones turned into mail art

ハーフサイズのカメラで写真撮影。河原での写真は露光が強すぎ焦点が合っていない。

送付された《石》のその後の姿を当時確認できたのは前山宛に送ったもののみ。GUN の郵送作品集に掲載するために前山の勤務地守門村（現魚沼市）の写真家に依頼して撮影した（Fig. 1.3）。以後、それを《石》の記録として様々な機会に活用してきた。

松澤宥宛の《石》は 2014 年に確認することができた（Fig. 1.4）。

1969.7.26
このメール・アートを送った直後に勤務校の生徒会誌第 51 号の「人類の月旅行に思う」というアポロ 11 号についての特集記事に寄稿する。

堀川紀夫「69721115620」
『高陵新報』51 号（1969 年 8 月 9 日）
あの時私は何をしていただろうか。アポロ 11 号が月に到達し月面に人間が降り立った時……。すばらしいイベントである。一言で言えば。しかし私個人の問題に還元してみた時、私は手をたたいて喜んではいられなかった。余りにも完全すぎた。余りにも美しすぎた。科学、いや人間の力の偉大さとともに、自分の力の無力を強く感じたのである。でも驚いてばかりいられない。私は月の石なんかには興味がない。このイベントをのりこえる思考を持とうそして、そこから新しく自己を見つめてみよう。視点を変えよう。思考の基底をかえよう。地球を月を水星をいや太陽系をいや銀河系を、もっと全宇宙をつつむ世界を考えよう。そして月の石を考えてみよう。世界は限りなく広い。その絶対的な広さを意識しよう。そしてその世界を外側からながめよう。

人間が月に立ち石を持ち帰ったところで宇宙は変わりはしない。変わるのは人間であり、思考である。

そして人間の物理的存在を考えよう。堀川という人間も宇宙の元素のある結びつきである。でも私は石でなかった。私は人間であった情念に満ちた。子供のように感動し、子供のように疑問を持とう。それが堀川が堀川であり人間である証明と言えよう。いろいろな面からものごとを考えようではないか。(7月26日)

---

is, 11 artists and art critics, including myself.

I cannot say that I am sure of its success, when I complete my mission at the post office. I cannot envision any future for my *Stones*.

After the mailing, I undertake the second stone gathering on that day with five former students of mine, now in their freshman year of high school, with whom I am friendly.

I use a half-frame camera to document the two stone gatherings. The resulting photographs are out of focus and overexposed.

At the time, I confirm the reception with only one addressee, Maeyama. Later that year, when we make *GUN: Niigata Contemporary Artists Collective*, a handmade mail-art booklet of GUN's works, we ask a photograph of the *Stone* from a photographer in Sumon village (present Uonuma city), where Maeyama was then teaching (Fig. 1.3). I have since used this photo as a document of *Stones* on various occasions.

Later, the reception of another *Stone*, sent to Matsuzawa Yutaka, is confirmed in 2014 (Fig. 1.4).

1969.7.26
Soon after the mailing, I contribute a text to a newsletter published by the student council of my school, for its special feature "Thinking on Human Travels to the Moon."

Horikawa Michio, "69721115620," *Kōryō shinpō* (Kōryō news), no. 51 (August 9, 1969) [J]
I am not interested in rocks on the moon. Let us conceive a thought that will transcend this event. And from there let us take a new look at ourselves. Let us change the foundation of our thinking. Let us think of a world that envelops Earth, the Moon, Mercury. No, the whole solar system. No, let us think of a world that envelops the whole universe. And let us think of the moon rocks. The world is infinitely vast. Let us be aware of this absolute vastness. And let us look at this world from the outside.

Nothing has changed in the universe even if humans stand on the moon and bring back moon rocks. What changes are humans, and their thinking.

And let us think about the physical existence of humankind. A human called Horikawa also represents a certain combination of elements within the universe. Yet I am not a stone. I am a human. Full of emotion and passion. Let us be moved like a child, let us question like a child. That proves that Horikawa is Horikawa and Horikawa is a human. (July 26)

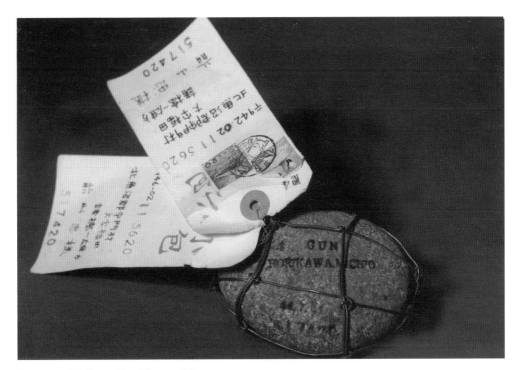

Fig. 1.3   *The Shinano River Plan: 11*, 1969
前山忠に送った《石》= *Stone* sent to Maeyama Tadashi

Fig. 1.4   *The Shinano River Plan: 11*, 1969
松澤宥に送った《石》= *Stone* sent to Matsuzawa Yutaka

1969.8 上旬
前山より、美術という幻想の終焉展のシンポジウムの
案内がある。その際に、前山が出席した現代国際彫刻
展のオープニングで《石》のことが話題に出たとの話
を聞いた。

1969.8.10
長野市信濃美術館で開催された美術という幻想の終焉
展のシンポジウムに行く。聴衆としてパネラーの発言
をメモする。

　　最後にあったフロアからの発言の機会に「会場の作
品は迫力ない」という意味の発言をしてしまう。松澤
宥から「あなたはどんなことをしているのですか」と
切り返され、「石を送る」ことをした、と発言。終わっ
て松澤と中原佑介に向かって会釈。

　　松澤の出品作品《お告げ》の青焼きコピーが会場に
数枚積まれていた。持ち帰り自由だったので1枚いた
だいて帰宅する。現在も大切に保管している。

1969.8.20
The Ara River Plan

夏季休暇で実家に帰省中であったので、近くの荒川（関
川の支流）で石を拾い、高田郵便局より発送、郵便料
260円。

1969.8.22
糸魚川市展で審査員の前田常作の評価により大光賞（大
光相互銀行協賛）を受賞した。また、法華経を学ぶよう
にとの助言を得る。

前田常作による公開審査・講評の後、15名ほどの参加
者全員が海を見に国道を横切って砂浜へ移動。そこに
横たわっていた大きな流木を見て、皆で力を合わせて
それを動かすハプニングをしようということになった。
前田も「初めての体験なので是非。一度はしてみたい
と思っていました」と言われて参加。時間はおおよそ
10分間。前田を先頭に、全員で心を一つに流木を高く
持ち上げる行為を行った。そのプロセスを撮影。

1969.8 (early month)
Maeyama Tadashi tells me about the symposium
related to *End of an Illusion That Is Art*, an exhibition at
Shinano Art Museum. He also tells me that he heard
people talking about my *Stones* when he attended the
opening of *Contemporary International Sculpture*.

1969.8.10
I attend the symposium related to *End of an Illusion That
Is Art* that Maeyama told me about. I make notes of the
panelists' words. At the very end, during a Q&A from
the audience, I make a comment, "The works in the
exhibition lack power," to which the artist Matsuzawa
Yutaka asks me, "What kind of work are you making?"
My response: "I mailed stones." After the proceedings,
I nod to Matsuzawa and the critic Nakahara Yūsuke.

　　I see a pile of blueprint copies of Matsuzawa's work
Message in the exhibition. They are made available
free for the audience to take, so I take one copy home,
which I still have in a good condition.

1969.8.20
The Ara River Plan
Number of stones sent: 1
Addressees

Sent to Itoigawa City Exhibition

I go home during the summer recess. I pick a stone at
the nearby Arakawa River (a tributary of the Seki River), and send it from the Takada Post Office. Postage is
260 yen.

1969.8.22
At *Itoigawa City Exhibition*, Maeda Jōsaku, a juror who
recognizes the *Stone*'s worth, is instrumental in grant-
ing me the Taikō Prize (sponsored by Taikō Mutual
Bank). He also advises me to study the Lotus Sutra.

After Maeda conducted his public selection and comment session, I and all other participants (altogether
15 or so) cross the national road to see the sea from a
sand beach. Upon seeing a large piece of driftwood, we
decide to do a Happening by moving it together. Saying
"This is my first experience, I long wanted to do [a
Happening]," Maeda joins us. We unite our minds and
together raise the wood high. I photograph the whole
process.

1968.8.25
I make my first data card for *Mail Art by Sending Stones*

1968.8.25

最初の《石》に関するデータカードを作成。生徒会誌への寄稿記事をコラージュし、石の重さ、送料、送付先を記載。勤務校のインクテープにムラのある和文タイプライターを使って作成した。写真は、荷造りの途中の1枚と、2回目の石拾いの3枚を密着プリントから切って貼った。2回目の石拾いに参加した高校1年生2名の証言を、後日10月11日に書き加えて完成 (Fig. 2)。

1969.8.27

The Shinano River Plan: 11-2

送付数：10

送付先

　山本孝（東京画廊）

　白田貞夫（シロタ画廊）

　宮澤壯佳（美術手帖編集長）

　並河恵美子（ルナミ画廊）

　川島良子（村松画廊）

　峯村敏明

　赤塚行雄

　三木多聞

　宮川淳

　清水楠男（南画廊）

糸魚川市展での受賞で、石を送るメール・アートが評価されそうな予感があり、7月21日のコンセプトでの第2の作品発表として発送した。荷札に The Shinano River Plan とタイトルを記入する。受け取り相手にインパクトを与えるために速達書留にした (Fig. 3.1)。データシートに郵便局の領収書を貼り込んだ。後日、12月に送付相手の2名（川島良子、白田貞夫）からサインをいただいた (Figs. 3.2–3)。

　清水楠男より受け取りのハガキをいただく。赤塚行雄よりコンセプチュアルな領収書作品2枚をいただく。

1969.9.7

Kiyotsu Canyon Plan

送付数：3

送付先

　赤瀬川原平

　中西夏之

　友人 K

(undertaken on July 21). I collage my essay published in the student council's newsletter as a main element. Around it, I type the weight of stones, postage, and addressees with a Japanese-language typewriter at school equipped with a worn ink ribbon. I also paste four frames from the contact sheets, one showing the prepared *Stones* and three from the second stone gathering on July 21. On October 11, I complete the card by adding witness accounts by two high-schoolers who participated in the second stone gathering (Fig. 2).

1969.8.27

The Shinano River Plan: 11-2

Number of stones sent: 10

Addressees

　Yamamoto Takashi (Tokyo Gallery)

　Shirota Sadao (Shirota Gallery)

　Miyazawa Takeyoshi (chief editor of *Bijutsu techō*)

　Namikawa Emiko (Lunami Gallery)

　Kawashima Yoshiko (Muramatsu Gallery)

　Minemura Toshiaki

　Akatsuka Yukio

　Miki Tamon

　Miyakawa Atsushi

　Shimizu Kusuo (Minami Gallery)

After receiving the prize at Itoigawa City Exhibition, I have a good feeling that my *Mail Art by Sending Stones* will gain recognition, and I undertake the second round of mailing based on the concept of July 21. This time, I include the title *The Shinano River Plan* on the mail tags. To enhance their impacts, I send them via registered express mail. I paste postal receipts on data cards (Fig. 3.1). In December, I have two recipients (Kawashima Yoshiko and Shirota Sadao) countersign the data cards (Figs. 3.2–3).

　I receive a postcard from Shimizu Kusuo acknowledging his reception. I also receive a pair of conceptual receipts from the critic Akatsuka Yukio.

1969.9.7

Kiyotsu Canyon Plan

Number of stones sent: 3

Addressees

　Akasegawa Genpei

　Nakanishi Natsuyuki

　K (a friend of mine)

On the way home from the Chūetsu Art Education Workshop at Kiyotsu Gorge Hot Spring in Nakasato village (present Tōkamachi city), I gather stones at the

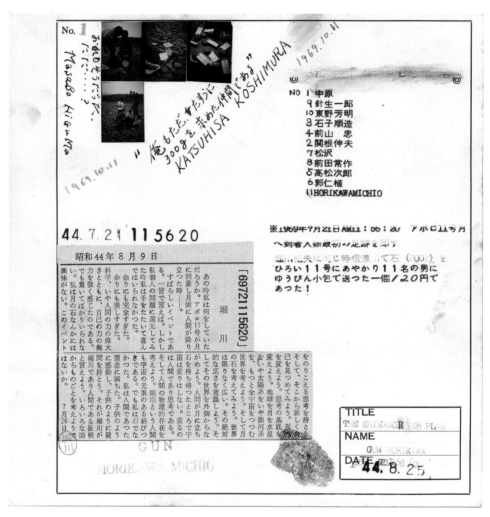

Fig. 2   *The Shinano River Plan: 11*, 1969

最初の《石》送付のデータカード = The very first data card of *Stone*

Fig. 3.1 *The Shinano River Plan: 11*, 1969
宮澤壯佳に送った《石》 = *Stone* sent to Miyazawa Takeyoshi

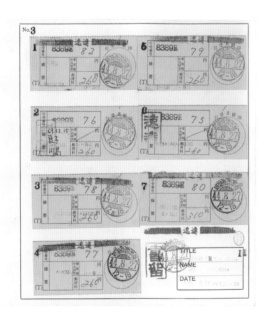 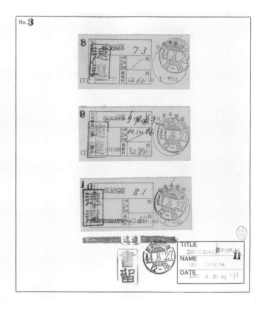

Fig. 3.2–3 *The Shinano River Plan: 11*, 1969
速達書留の領収書を貼り込んだデータカード = Data cards with receipts for registered express mail

中里村（現十日町市）の清津峡温泉で開催された中越美術教育研修会の帰りに清津川で採取した石を送る。小さな石でコンセプトが観光地宣伝のようになってしまった。失敗作である。

1969.10.13–11.13

このひと月の間に10種類のハガキ・アートを48名に送る。ハガキ実物、郵便局のレシート、送付先リストが残されている。

　速達だけ、ハガキ面を黒塗り、切手を1円追加、ハガキ裏を表に使用、官製ハガキの代金表示のところに同じ金額の切手を貼る、表を裏から見た図を裏に印刷、官製ハガキの周囲を1ミリカット、官製ハガキの切手印刷部分を切って2倍の切手を貼って送る、官製ハガキの切手の大きさを切って穴を開けて2倍の切手で送る、書留だけの10種類。

1969.11

『美術手帖』編集長・宮澤壮佳に送った《石》の写真が掲載されて批評される。

李禹煥「観念の芸術は可能か：オブジェ思想の正体とゆくえ」『美術手帖』

新潟のある作家から、書留で「石」が送られてきた。こぶしほどの石を、細い針金で縛り付けた「作品」である。別段、特殊な石には見えず、ただそこらにころがっていそうなものだが、わざわざ針金で縛りつけた作家の意図物ということで、受け取る人間は、否応なしにまざまざとこれを見やったりさわったりせざるを得ない。そして、どう見てもこれはただの「石」であり、それ以上でも以下で以外でもない、「定められた石」であるに過ぎないことを再確認する。そこで、ということは逆に、これは不確定的な自然な石自身としての石にあらず、その実、送り主の観念の凝固物という形においての「石」であることに次第に気づくのである。「石」は、石を語らず送り主の観念を示すだけのものになっているからだろう（70頁）。

1969.11.4

The Shinano River Plan No. 3

送付数：1

Kiyotsu River and send them out. The act of sending these small stones is tantamount to tourism promotion. It is a failure.

1969.10.13–11.13

Over the period of a month, I send 10 kinds of postcard art to 48 people. The mailing is documented by the postcard specimens, post office receipts, and the list of addresses.

I devise 10 types of postcard modification and mailing variations: 1) to send via express mail; 2) to paint the text side black; 3) to attach a one-yen stamp in addition; 4) to use the text side for address; 5) to attach a stamp in the amount of postcard rate over the preprinted stamp of a post office–issued postcard; 6) to print a backside view of the address side on the text side (as though seen through from the text side); 7) to trim 1 millimeter from each side of a post office–issued postcard; 8) to cut out the preprinted stamp from a post office–issued postcard and add stamps in twice the amount of the regular postcard rate; 9) to cut a stamp-shaped hole in the blank area and add stamps in twice the amount of the regular rate; 10) to mail as registered mail.

1969.11

The *Stone* I sent to Miyazawa Takeyoshi, Chief Editor of *Bijutsu techō*, is illustrated and criticized in the beginning of an essay published in his magazine.

Lee Ufan, "Is an Art of *Kannen* Possible? The Truth and Future of the *Objet* Thought," *Bijutsu techō* [J]
An artist in Niigata sent me a "stone" by registered mail. It's a "work," wherein a fist-sized stone was bound by thin wires. Honestly speaking, it doesn't look like any special stone, just the kind you can see lying around somewhere. Since the artist demonstrated his intention by binding it with wires, the recipient is, like it or not, compelled to look at it or touch it also intently. Yet, we have to confirm that no matter how we see it, this is a mere "stone," nothing more and nothing less, just a "predetermined stone." Thus—or nevertheless—we gradually understand that it is not a stone as such existing namelessly in nature, but a "stone" that embodies the "consolidation of the sender's *hannen* (idea)." That is perhaps because the "stone" becomes nothing but an object that points to the sender's idea, instead of revealing stone-ness (p. 70).

送付先

十日町市展に出品

1969.11.14–24

アポロ 12 号 打ち上げ、月面着陸、船外活動、地球帰
還

1969.11.20

The Shinano River Plan: 12

送付数：12

送付先

李禹煥

山本孝

清水楠男

東野芳明

前田常作

宮澤壯佳

石子順造

中原佑介

針生一郎

瀧口修造

1969.11.4

The Shinano River Plan No. 3

Number of stones sent: 1

Addressees

Sent to Tōkamachi City Exhibition

1969.11.14–24

**The Apollo 12 mission encompasses its launch,
lunar landing, extravehicular activities on the lunar
surface, and flight home.**

1969.11.20

The Shinano River Plan: 12

Number of stones sent: 12

Addressees

Lee Ufan

Yamamoto Takashi

Shimizu Kusuo

Tōno Yoshiaki

Maeda Jōsaku

Miyazawa Takeyoshi

Ishiko Junzō

Nakahara Yūsuke

Haryū Ichirō

Takiguchi Shūzō

横尾忠則

瀬木慎一

アポロ 12 号にちなみ、石 12 個を採取し、それを石屋
で二つに切断して一方を送り、もう一方を河原に返す
試みをした。一番大きな石の半分は実物記録として手
元に残した。

　石の半分はアートになり、半分は川原に永遠に残り
続けるという物語の生成を意図した（Figs. 4.1–3）。

　石屋と郵便局の領収書をデータカードに貼り込み、
後日東京でお目にかかる機会があった時に、石子順造、
李禹煥（1969.12.15）と前田常作、中原佑介、山本孝（1970.5.8,
10, 12）の 5 人より受け取りの確認を兼ねて署名をいた
だいた（Figs . 4.4–5）。

　清水楠男より受け取りのハガキをいただく。

1969.11

前田常作から紹介をいただき、上京して新宿椿近代画
廊で稲憲一郎、竹田潔らと会う。「精神生理学研究所」
と名付けられたメール・アートのグループ活動に参加
することになる。決められた日時の行為、無行為の記

Yokoo Tadanori

Segi Shin'ichi

In conjunction with the Apollo 12 mission, I collect 12
stones, have them split into halves, and mail one half of
each out. Among the remaining other halves, I keep the
largest one, and return the rest to the Shinano River.
I envision a story that a set of stone halves become art,
and the other halves forever remain on the dry riverbed
(Figs. 4.1–3).

　I paste the stone-cutter's receipts and postal
receipts on data cards. Later in December 1969 and
May 1970, I have a chance to meet five recipients, who
countersign the data cards. They are: Ishiko Junzō, Lee
Ufan, Maeda Jōsaku, Nakahara Yūsuke, and Yamamoto
Takashi (Figs. 4.4–5).

　I receive a postcard acknowledging the reception of
a *Stone* from Sh imizu Kusuo.

1969.11

Maeda Jōsaku gives me a letter of introduction to Ina
Ken'ichirō and Taked a Kiyoshi. I meet with them at
Tsubaki Kindai Gallery in Tokyo. I decide to participate
in their mail-art collective Psychophysiology Research
Institute (Seishin Seirigaku Kenkyūjo), a project to col-

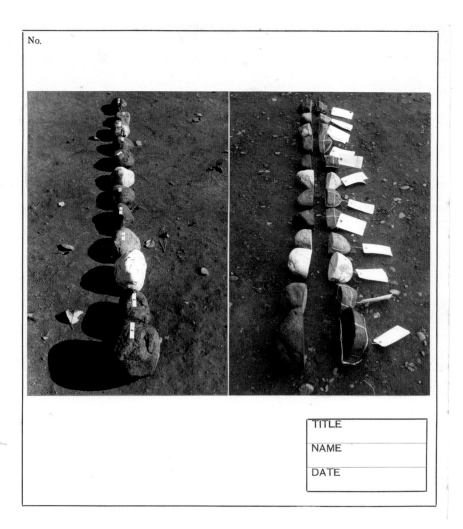

Fig. 4.1 *The Shinano River Plan: 12*, 1969
石の採集、切断、河原への返却、郵送をコンセプト化したデータカード
= Data card showing the concept of gathering, cutting, returning to the dry riverbed, and mailing of *Stones*

Fig. 4.2   *The Shinano River Plan: 12*, 1969
宮澤壯佳に送った《石》= *Stone* sent to Miyazawa Takeyoshi

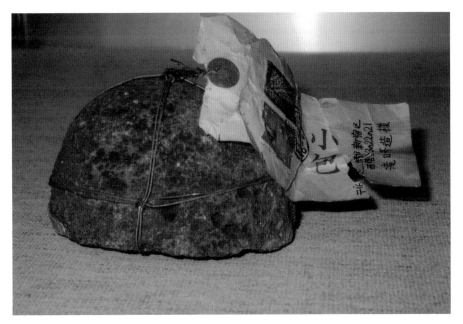

Fig. 4.3   *The Shinano River Plan: 12*, 1969
瀧口修造に送った《石》= *Stone* sent to Takiguchi Shūzō

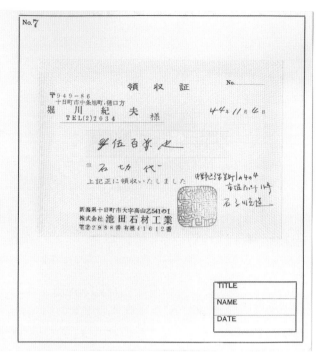

Fig. 4.4   *The Shinano River Plan: 12*, 1969
石屋の領収書に石子順造が署名したデータカード
= Data card with a stone cutter's receipt, later signed by Ishiko Junzō

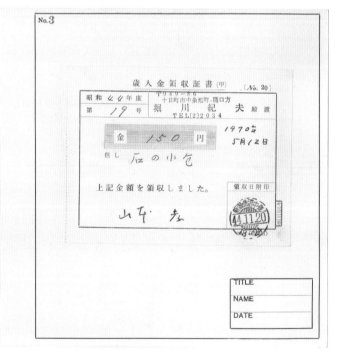

Fig. 4.5   *The Shinano River Plan: 12*, 1969
郵便局の領収書に山本孝が署名したデータカード
= Data card with a post-office receipt, later signed by Yamamoto Takashi

録を結集して50名ほどの相手に送り届けることで成立させた「見えない美術館」の活動だった。

その最初の活動日は12月7日。その日に米国のアポロ計画の最高責任者であるニクソン大統領に航空便で《石》を送付した。前衛的アートのグループ活動として目立つことが肝要と考えて事に及んでしまったわけである。

1969.12.7
The Shinano River Plan "Christmas Present"
送付数：1
送付先
　　米国ホワイトハウスのニクソン大統領

第1回精神生理学研究所の活動として実施する（Fig. 5.1）。十日町郵便局でこの発送手続きをしている場面を企業キャンペーンで十日町市に来訪中の写真家・羽永光利が撮影（Fig. 5.2）。

1969.12
GUNと羽永光利との交流から国道253号線の十日町橋近くの河原で《雪に顔料をまくイベント》の構想が実現に向かって動き始める。

1969.12.31
郵送作品集『新潟現代美術家集団GUN』の手作り冊子を郵送発表（参加者5名）、30部くらい発行。前山に送った最初の《石》の写真、石をカットしたことを示すコンセプト写真、ニクソン大統領に送った際のレシートを発表する。

1970.1.8
「大統領に石贈ろう」
『読売新聞』全国版「第三の若者」シリーズ

羽永光利から「ニクソン大統領に石を送った話」が読売新聞社社会部に伝わり、電話で1時間以上の取材を受けることに発展した。取材される過程で「石を送る行為」に込めた意味が物語となり記事が実現した（Fig. 6）。

1970.1.23
米国駐日大使から「大統領へ石を送った」ことへの礼状を受け取る。読売新聞に出た記事を見ての反応と

---

lect acts and non-acts undertaken at a specified date and time and circulate them among 50 or so recipients.

Its first day of action is December 7, for which I decide to send a *Stone* to U.S. President Nixon, the supreme commander of the Apollo project. I think it important that I must do something eye-catching for the activity of a vanguard collective.

1969.12.7
The Shinano River Plan "Christmas Present"
Number of stones sent: 1
Addressees
　　U.S. President Richard Nixon at the White House

I undertake this mailing as my first act for Psychophysiology Research Institute (Fig. 5.1). The scene at the Tōkamachi Post Office is photographed by the photographer Hanaga Mitsutoshi, who is visiting the city on assignment for a corporate PR campaign (Fig. 5.2).

1969.12
The exchange between GUN and Hanaga Mitsutoshi leads to the project idea for "an event to spread pigments over the snow" on a dry riverbed near the Tōkamachi Bridge on National Route 253 and we begin preparation.

1969.12.31
We mail *GUN: Niigata Contemporary Artists Collective*, a handmade mail-art booklet of GUN's works. With the participation of 5 members, some 30 copies are produced. My work is represented by a photo of the first *Stone* sent to Maeyama, a concept photo that demonstrates the halving of 12 *Stones*, and the postage receipt for mailing a *Stone* to President Nixon.

1970.1.8
"Let's Send a Stone to President," *Yomiuri shinbun*, national edition, "Third Youth" series [J]

Hanaga Mitsutoshi tells the episode of my sending a *Stone* to President Nixon to the Mainichi newspaper's Social Desk, which decides to interview me. During the interview, over an hour, I articulate the meaning in the act of sending stones, which forms the core of the published article (Fig. 6).

1970.1.23
I receive a thank-you note from the American Ambassador in Tokyo. I think it is a reaction to the Yomiuri

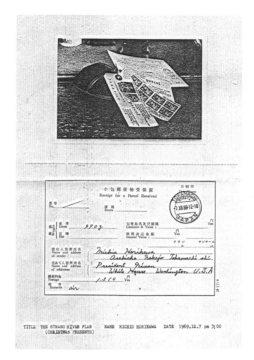

Fig. 5.1   *The Shinano River Plan: "Christmas Present,"* 1969
『精神生理学研究所』(ポートフォリオ版1970年)に収録されたデータカード
= Data card included in *Psychophysiology Research Institute* (portfolio, 1970) *Stone*

Fig. 5.2   *The Shinano River Plan: "Christmas Present,"* 1969
十日町郵便局でニクソン大統領へ送付手続き
= Sending *Stone* to President Nixon at Tōkamachi Post Office

遊びのハプニング

第三の若者

郵便局員がビックリしたニクソン大統領へのプレゼント（12月7日、十日町市の郵便局で。右が堀川先生）

⑦

大統領に石贈ろう

「メール・アート」先生

信濃川川原に立つ

HORIKAWA "MICHIO" 堀川紀

"MR&S プレゼント"

昨年暮れ、ワシントンのホワイトハウスに、おかしなクリスマ

ス・プレゼントが届いた。

荷札が三枚。あて名は「PRESIDENT NIXON」。

さし出し人の「MICHIO HORIKAWA」――堀川紀

おとなのこぶし大、むき出しの黒い石ころ。しばった針金に、そえ書きもないので、余白に

オレたちも、石を拾ってみよう。

制作費二万円ナリ

『地球の石』の意味

夫さん（三）は、織物の町・新潟県十日町市、中条中学校の美術担当教論。一昨年春、新潟大を卒業と同時に、この学校に勤めている。

昨年七月二十一日昼。月面に着陸したアポロ11号のアームストロング船長が、人間の小さな一歩〝を踏んだとき、堀川先生は授業中の一年A組の生徒たちにこういった。

「アームストロング船長とおれと、どっちが、これから先〝の石を拾う。遠く離れた地球の石だ」

こうして、十二月七日、堀川先生と生徒たちが信濃川川原で拾った石を、ニクソン大統領へ送った。

Fig. 6 *The Shinano River Plan: "Christmas Present,"* 1969

　　　『読売新聞』全国版「第三の若者⑦」（1970年1月8日付）

　　　= "Third Youth" series, Yomiuri shinbun, national edition, January 8, 1970

思われた。曰く「ニクソン大統領は、非常に稀なクリスマスプレゼントを送ってくださった貴殿の思慮深さに非常なる感謝の意を伝えてほしいと、私に依頼されました」（Fig. 7）。米国のユーモア感覚と懐の深さに感心する。

1970.2.11+15
新潟現代美術家集団 GUN の《雪のイメージを変えるイベント》に参加。これが『アサヒグラフ』3月6日号と『芸術生活』4月号で紹介され、全国発信となる。

　羽永光利は4色の顔料の調達に尽力するとともに、そのイベントを写真家の仕事として公式に撮影。撮影者はもう一人磯俊一がいた。

　私はこのイベントの際に参加者集団で顔料を振りまいて巨大な抽象画を描いた後、一人でふんどし一丁の姿で赤い顔料を散布するパフォーマンスを行い、大いに目立つこととなった。

1970.3
この時点で《石を送るメール・アート》と《雪のイメージを変えるイベント》で日本のアートの前衛を走って

いたように内心思っていた。

「デザインはもともと匿名的なものだ　横尾忠則——非連続の連続によるインタビュー」『美術手帖』
冒頭に《石》が話に出る（96頁）。

1970.3.9
The Shinano River Plan
送付数：1
送付先
　稲憲一郎

1970.3.31
横浜こどもの国での現代美術フェスティバルに参加。前山忠と連名でエントリー。作品は前山が制作した反戦ポスター作品。そのオープニングの日に中原佑介に声をかけられ、第10回東京ビエンナーレ：人間と物質展に招待の話をいただく。その際「展覧会では郵送も含めた多様なメディアを使いたい」との話しがあった。

---

article. It says, "President Nixon has asked me to convey his great appreciation for your thoughtfulness in sending him a most unusual Christmas gift" (Fig. 7). I am very impressed by the American sense of humor and open-mindedness.

1970.2.11, 15
I participate in GUN's *Event to Change the Image of Snow*. The information about it is transmitted nationwide, with photographs of the project published in two magazines, *Asahi Graph* (March 6) and *Geijutsu seikatsu* (April).

Hanaga was instrumental in procuring four colors of pigment and acted as our official photographer to document the acts. Another photographer present was Iso Toshikazu. Together with a group of participants, I create a gigantic abstract painting by spraying pigments over the snow. Afterwards, I make a splashy undertaking of a solo performance of spraying red pigments over snow, all naked except for a loincloth.

1970.3
Around this time, I secretly think that I am a frontrunner of vanguard art in Japan with my *Mail Art by Sending Stones* and GUN's *Event to Change the Image of Snow*.

"Design Is Anonymous to Begin With: Yokoo Tadanori's Uncontinuously Continuous Interview," published in *Bijutsu techō* [J]

My *Stone* I sent to Yokoo is discussed in the beginning of the interview (p. 96).

1970.3.9
The Shinano River Plan
Number of stones sent: 1
Addressees
　Ina Ken'ichirō

1970.3.31
Jointly with Maeyama Tadashi, I enter a work (Maeyama's antiwar poster) in *Contemporary Art Festival* at the Kodomo no Kuni amusement park in Yokohama. At the opening, Nakahara Yūsuke stops me to discuss my participation in *Tokyo Biennale 1970: Between Man and Matter*, indicating he wants to see "the use of various mediums, including mail art."

1970.4
Tōno Yoshiaki, "My Study," *Chūō kōron* [J]

EMBASSY OF THE
UNITED STATES OF AMERICA

Tokyo, Japan

January 23, 1970

Mr. Michio Horikawa
Yuji-Higuchi House
Asahi-cho Nakajo
Tokamachi-shi
Niigata-ken, Japan

Dear Mr. Horikawa:

President Nixon has asked me to convey his
great appreciation for your thoughtfulness in sending
him a most unusual Christmas gift.

Sincerely,

Armin H. Meyer
American Ambassador

Fig. 7   *The Shinano River Plan: "Christmas Present,"* 1969
アメリカ大使からの感謝状 = A thank-you note from the American Ambassador

1970.4

東野芳明「私の書斎」『中央公論』

書棚に横に置かれた『マルセル・デュシャン語録』の上にアポロ12号の際に送った《石》が置かれている写真が掲載される（Fig. 8）。

1970.4.1

十日町市立中条中学校から高田市立（現・上越市）中ノ俣中学校へ転勤となる。中ノ俣は市内より13 kmくらい西側に入った山間僻地。

1970.4.9

東京ビエンナーレ参加プランを立案。勤務校集落に流れる中ノ俣川でアポロ13号飛行計画に因み、打ち上げ予定の12日に13個の自然石を採集して郵送する構想。タイトルを The Nakanomata River Plan: 13 とすることをカタログ原稿とともに国際展事務局へ送る。

1970.4.12

アポロ13号打ち上げられる。

1970.4.13–25

The Nakanomata River Plan: 13

送付数：13

送付先

　　東京ビエンナーレ：人間と物質展に出品

出品作品の最初の行為として、4月12日に集落に流れる中ノ俣川で13個の石を拾う。

　4月13日から1日1個、毎日新聞国際展事務局あてへ郵送を開始する。1日1個という送り方は集落から徒歩で市の中心部にある本局まで郵便物を運ぶ配達員小林武雄への配慮もあった。

　提出した計画には29日に「パネルに記録記入完成」と記していたが、特製のカードをシルク印刷しそこに記録を記入する方式に変更。展覧会後にそれを封筒に引かれた破線を切るとアーティスト・ブックのように読める体裁に仕立てて限定3部の記録集とした（Fig. 9）。

1970.4.15

アポロ13号は、飛行途中に機械船の酸素タンク1個が爆発。この事故によりミッション中止を余儀なくさ

In the photograph of Tōno's bookshelves, my *Stone*, which I sent him in conjunction with Apollo 12, is placed on the Japanese translation of *To and from Rrose Selavy: Selected Words of Marcel Duchamp* (trans. Takiguchi Shūzō, 1968) (Fig. 8).

1970.4.1

I transfer from Tōkamachi City Nakajō Middle School to Takada (presently Jōetsu) City Nakanomata Middle School. Nakanomata is located 13 kilometers west of downtown Takada in a remote mountain area.

1970.4.9

I make a plan for my participation in *Tokyo Biennale 1970*. In conjunction with the Apollo 13 mission, I will gather 13 stones on April 12, the scheduled day of launch, at the Nakanomata River flowing in the village that my school served. They will be mailed from a local post office under the title *The Nakanomata River Plan: 13*. I send the plan to the exhibition office, together with the material for the exhibition catalogue.

1970.4.12

Apollo 13 is launched.

1970.4.13–25

*The Nakanomata River Plan: 13**

Number of stones sent: 13

Addressees

　　Sent to *Tokyo Biennale 1970: Between Man and Matter*

　　* Editor's note: Horikawa undertook four stone mailings for the exhibition, which was shown in four different venues, in Tokyo, Kyoto, Nagoya, and Fukuoka. For the second mailing onward, he only sent 9 stones, as will be explained below (1970.5.10–31).

On April 12, I initiate my participation in the exhibition by gathering 13 stones at the Nakanomata River that flows through the village.

　From April 13 onward, I send 1 *Stone* to the exhibition office every day. The method of sending 1 *Stone* a day is devised partly in consideration of Kobayashi Takeo, a postman who has to carry the mail bag on foot from the village to the Central Post Office at Takada's city center.

　In the original plan I sent to the exhibition office, I wrote that I would "finish recording the data on panels" on April 29, but I change my mind and use specially designed silkscreened cards. After the exhibition, I

Fig. 8   *The Shinano River Plan: 12*, 1969
『中央公論』1970 年 4 月号に掲載された《石》
= *Stone* reproduced in *Chūō kōron* (April 1970)

Fig. 9   *The Shinano River Plan: 13*, 1970
東京ビエンナーレの《石》のデータカードの 1 枚（13 頁）
= One of the data cards for *Tokyo Biennale* (p. 13)

れ、危機を乗り越えて乗組員全員が 17 日に無事に地球へ帰還した。

1970.4 下旬
アポロ 13 号計画は頓挫するが、《The Nakanomata River Plan: 13》は 25 日に無事終了した。そして、月面探査計画に対応する《石を送るメール・アート》のコンセプトは変更を余儀なくされた。

1970.5.3
The Shinano River Plan (for peace of world)
送付数：1
送付先
　佐藤栄作総理

東京ビエンナーレに参加する若い作家として、毎日新聞より 5 月 1 日付ウナ電報で「ニヒルマエマイニチシンブ ンシャカイブ アリマサントシャシンブ ナカオサンガ シュザ イニユキマスガ ッコウデ オマチコウナオ三ヒモアケテオイテクダ サイ」ミネムラ（峯村敏明）の取材依頼。

2 日に残雪の残る山道を歩いて来た記者 2 人を迎え、中ノ俣川で石を拾う様子の撮影を試みる。もっと眺望の良いところで撮影したいとの要望が出て、翌 3 日に中ノ俣から前任地十日町市の信濃川まで出向いて石を拾い、針金を巻き、魚沼中条郵便局から郵送する一連の行為を取材、撮影していただく。この年はかなりの豪雪で、河原にまだ雪が残っていた (Figs. 10.1–3)。

この機会を第 6 回精神生理学研究所の活動と位置づける。

1970.5.9
東京都美術館へ出向いて送り届けた《石》と対面。展示作業進行中の会場を回り、他の作家とバッティングしないように配慮して会場内の 13 箇所の床に《石》を置き、田中信太郎作品の部屋の壁に最新機器のゼロックスでコピーした 13 枚の記録カードを横に並べて展示する (Figs. 11.1–3)。

会場の東京都美術館前でリチャード・セラが鉄輪を設置するためにツルハシを振り上げている現場を目撃し 5 枚くらい写真撮影する。友人の稲憲一郎らが搬出入業者としてその現場でアルバイトをしていた。

---

create three editions of a mail-art artist book by collating them in an envelope. The recipient may cut open the envelope along the cut-here lines and read the contents like an artist book (Fig. 9).

1970.4.15
An oxygen tank of Apollo 13 explodes. This accident forces the mission to be terminated. The entire crew overcome the difficulties and return safely home to the earth on April 17.

1970.4 (late month)
Although the Apollo 13 mission is terminated midway through, I successfully complete *The Nakanomata River Plan: 13* on April 25. However, I am compelled to modify my original concept of countering the extravehicular activities on the lunar surface by my *Mail Art by Sending Stones*.

1970.5.3
The Shinano River Plan (for peace of world)
Number of stones sent: 1
Addressees
　Prime Minister Satō Eisaku

I receive an interview request from Minemura Toshiaki via express telegram dated May 1: "[On] second, before noon, Mainichi newspaper social-desk reporter Mr. Arima and photographer Mr. Nakaoka visit you. Please wait at school. Please keep third open."

On May 2, I receive the two, who walked a mountain path covered by the leftover snow. They try to photograph me picking stones at the Nakanomata River. They want to photograph me in a more scenic area, so we decide to go on the next day to the Shinano River at Tōkamachi, where I used to teach before Nakanomata. They document a series of my acts: picking a stone, binding it with wires, and mailing it from the Uonuma Nakajō Post Office. The snow this year is very deep, with leftover snow visible on the dry riverbed (Figs. 10.1–3).

I make this as the 6th act of Psychophysiology Research Institute.

1970.5.9
I go to Tokyo Metropolitan Art Museum to meet with my *Stones* which I mailed to the exhibition office. With all the installation activities taking place in the museum, I carefully select 13 spots to place my *Stones* without disturbing other artists' displays. I install 13 data

Fig. 10.1   *The Shinano River Plan (for piece of world)*, 1970
毎日新聞社の取材で佐藤栄作首相に送る《石》の採集を撮影
= Gathering of a *Stone* for prime minister Satō Eisaku is photographed by a Mainichi cameraman on May 3

Fig. 10.2   *The Shinano River Plan (for piece of world)*, 1970
Vサインはベトナム反戦平和運動など反体制的行動のファッションだった
= Flashing a V sign, a popular antiestablishment gesture during the time of the anti-Vietnam peace movement

Fig. 10.3　*The Shinano River Plan (for piece of world)*, 1970
　　　　　　教え子たちが郵送の場面を見学に来てくれた = My students witnessing my mailing at the post office

Fig. 11.1　*The Shinano River Plan 13*, 1970
　　　　　　東京ビエンナーレで床に展示された《石》
　　　　　　= *Stone* on the floor at *Tokyo Biennale*

Fig. 11.2   *The Shinano River Plan: 13*, 1970
東京ビエンナーレでダニエル・ビュランの部屋に展示された《石》
= *Stone* shown in Daniel Buren's room at *Tokyo Bienale*

Fig. 11.3   *The Shinano River Plan: 13*, 1970
東京ビエンナーレで展示された《石》= *Stone* shown at *Tokyo Biennale*

1970.5.10–31

第10回東京ビエンナーレ：人間と物質展がオープンする。私はいきなり国際的な舞台に立つことになったが正直言って外国の作家で知っていたのはクリストとバリー・フラナガンの2人だけだった。初めて見る作家たちの先端的、概念的、多様な表現の数々が記憶の深部に刻印され、自分のアート認識の狭さ、浅学、経験不足を強く思い知らされた。

その後、東京都美術館での会期中4個の作品が会場から姿を消す。同展が名古屋、京都、福岡に巡回した際、13個から東京会場で無くなった4個分を引いて各会場（事務局）に9個ずつ石を送る。なお、巡回展の会場へ見に行くことは当時の交通事情と本業勤務の多忙さ等で不可能だった。

東京ビエンナーレ展関連記事より ────────

1970.4.30

安井収蔵「第10回東京ビエンナーレ『人間と物質』に迫る」『毎日新聞』

堀川紀夫（新潟）の"作品"は行為である。その行為はすでに四月二十日からはじまっている。住まいの近くを流れる小川で、彼は毎日一個の石を拾う。その状況を記録し、ハリガネで包みトウキョウ・ビエンナーレ事務局へ書留郵便で送り続けている。こうして十三日間にわたって十三個の石を送り続ける。五月十日の開会式に彼は上京しその十三個の石を確認する。こうした行為によって、彼は自身と社会とのかかわりあいを確かめるのである。

1970.5.14

「若ものたち〈25〉」『毎日新聞』

5月2、3日の写真取材をもとにした記事が出る。《炭》を出品した成田克彦と2人で取り上げられた（Fig. 12）。

---

cards, reproduced on the latest Xerox machine, side by side on a wall of Tanaka Shintarō's room (Figs. 11.1–3).

In front of the museum, I witness Richard Serra working with a pickaxe in order to install his iron ring in the ground. I take five or so shots of him. I notice Serra's crew includes Ina Ken'ichirō, a friend of mine, as a parttime handler.

1970.5.10–31

Tokyo Biennale 1970: Between Man and Matter opens. All of a sudden, I find myself standing on an international stage. Honestly speaking, I know of only two foreign artists there, Christo and Barry Flanagan. I come to realize how lacking I was in my understanding, knowledge, and experience of art, as I absorb the innovative, conceptual, and diverse expressions of those artists I see for the first time.

During the exhibition, 4 of my *Stones* disappear. When the exhibition travels to Nagoya, Kyoto, and Fukuoka, I send 9 *Stones* (13 minus 4) to each local exhibition office. Due to my busy schedule at school and the difficulty of travel at the time, I cannot visit the three exhibition venues.

Selected Press Reports of *Tokyo Biennale* ────────

1970.4.30

Yasui Shūzō, "Confronting 10th Tokyo Biennale: Between Man and Matter," *Mainichi shinbun* [J]

Horikawa Michio's (Niigata) "work" is his acts. They began already on April 20. At a small stream near his home, he picked a stone a day, wound it with wires, and sent it by registered mail to the Tokyo Biennale office. He thus sent 13 stones over the period of 13 days. He came to Tokyo for the exhibition's opening ceremony and confirmed [the reception of] his 13 stones. Through these acts, he confirmed his relationship with society.

1970.5.14

"Young People (25)," *Mainichi shinbun* [J]

Article is based on the photographing session on May 2–3. I am featured together with Narita Katsuhiko, who exhibited *Charcoal* in *Tokyo Biennale 1970* (Fig. 12).

1970.5.22

"From *10th Tokyo Biennale*," *Niigata nippō* [J]

Here and there, you can see stones lying on the floor.

Fig. 12   *The Shinano River Plan (for piece of world)*, 1970
この写真が記事に掲載された = This photo illustrated in Mainichi article

1970.5.22

「第十回日本国際美術展から」『新潟日報』

会場のところどころに石が落ちている。しかし、これは片づけ忘れた石ではなくて、堀川紀夫の作品であった。彼は何の変哲もない石ころ十三個を一日一個ずつ十三日がかりで国際美術展の事務局へ書留・速達で送り、置き場所も指定した。

1970.6

中原佑介「今月の焦点：人間と物質のふれあい」
『美術手帖』

堀川は、石を裸のまま郵送し、コミュニケイションそのものを、新しい体験とし直そうとする試みを続けてきた。(127頁)

1970.6

羽永光利「体制裏の芸術家〈3〉」
『詩と芸術の総合誌ぴろえた』

「もの」の意味を探る芸術家

アポロ11号が月に着陸して、石を採取した頃、堀川紀夫は新潟県十日町市、信濃川の河原で、こぶし大の石を、拾い集めた。彼の行為には、月に行って石を採る作業と地球上で石を拾う行為とはまったく同じ次元に他ならないという観点であり、アポロが地球に向って石を運んで帰る時間に合わせて、堀川紀夫は、石に、はり金を巻き荷札を付けて知人に発送した。その一つはニクソン大統領にも送付されたのである。彼の発想の中には「月からもって帰る石によって、地球の比重は微小ながら変わるのであるから、地球の石を、その持ち帰った石の重量だけ、次の月に向かう宇宙船で運び込むべきだ」という考えがあった。ニクソンからは、メイヤー米大使を通じてクリスマスプレゼントとして受け取ったというメッセージを受け取った。彼自身はいささか意図が通じなかったのに、不満のようであったが、彼の広大な展望には、美術とか、芸術とかのジャンルに埋没しないものがあった。むしろ、私たちの至極、日常的な生活で、忘れ去られた、或いは忘れようとしている、発想の「もの」の、とらえ方を見出すことが出来る。堀川は、五月十日から都美術館で行われた人間と物質展に参加しているが、あの巨大な箱の中で、彼の展望がどこまで見られるだろうか、それ

It's not that somebody failed to put them away, but Horikawa Michio put them there as his work. Every day, over 13 days, he picked one insignificant small stone and sent it via registered express mail to the Tokyo Biennale office. He also specified where to place them.

1970.6

Nakahara Yūsuke, "Focus of This Month: Encounter between Man and Matter," *Bijutsu techō* [J]
Horikawa mailed stones without wrapping them in paper. In doing so, he has tried to explore a new experience of communication itself (p. 127).

1970.6

Hanaga Mitsutoshi, "Artists behind the Establishment (3)," *Piroeta: A Journal of Poetry and Art* [J]
An Artist Exploring the Meaning of "Things"
When Apollo 11 landed on the moon and collected rock specimens, Horikawa Michio collected fist-sized stones gathered by the bed of the Shinano River in Tōkamachi, Niigata Prefecture. In his logic, the rock gathering on the moon is on par [in terms of significance] with the stone gathering on the earth. He timed his act of mailing his stones wound with wires and tagged with mailing labels in parallel to Apollo 11's return home with the moon rocks. One of his stones was sent to President Nixon. He thought, "The rocks brought back from the moon change the weight of the earth, even slightly, so we should bring earth stones of the same weight on the next mission to the moon." Nixon sent the artist a message, via American Ambassador Meyer in Tokyo, that he had received Horikawa's stone as a gift. However, the artist appears unsatisfied that the American president had understood his intention. Still, Horikawa's vast vision transcended the confines of art. Rather, from his act, we can see a way to inspire through "things" that were forgotten or are being forgotten in our very mundane life. From May 10, Horikawa participated in *Tokyo Biennale 1970: Between Man and Matter* held at Tokyo Metropolitan Art Museum. In that huge box, how much of his vision can be seen? At the same time, it will raise a question about the future of the museum (p. 104).

1970.6.1

"Art as Brain Gymnastics: Visitors 'Tackle' *Tokyo Biennale*," *Shūkan Bunshun* [J]

はまた今後の都美術館のありようが問われる、問題の提起にもなるはずだからであろう。(104頁)

1970.6.1
「芸術・頭の体操：東京ビエンナーレ展と "取り組む" 入場者たち」『週刊文春』
10枚の組写真の中で、観客が腰を曲げて床の上の《石》を見ている写真が掲載された (Fig. 13)。

1970.6.7
岡田隆彦「鑑賞席 新しい言葉を求めて」『朝日ジャーナル』
唯一のカット写真に取り上げられて、「河原でひろった石を小包にして郵送したものを会場のあちこちに置いているもの」というコメントがついた (34頁)。

1970.6.14
「新しい試みの『東京ビエンナーレ』」『サンデー毎日』
たとえば新潟県高田市の川でひろった十三個の石を、番号順に書留速達で送り それを指定の場所に展示する(堀川紀夫)といった作品もある。

1970.6.20
『若者の生きがい 一度しかない青春のために』
読売新聞・社会部編 エール出版社刊
「キミも "郵送芸術" に参加しよう "遊び" の価値を探求するグループ」に掲載される (91–99頁)。

1970 summer
ジョーゼフ・P・ラブ「第10回東京ビエンナーレ」『アート・インターナショナル』[E]
作品写真が冒頭 (70頁) に掲載される (Fig. 14)。

1970.7
峯村敏明 (図版解説)「これが なぜ芸術か 第10回東京ビエンナーレを機に」『美術手帖』
堀川から石がおくられてきたとき、郵便配達夫が受取人にいった「お若いのにいい趣味をおもちですな」。堀川はもっぱら身近な生活状況の中で、人間の行為の意味を掘り起こそうと考えて石を拾い、友人に送りつける。石そのものにどのような意味も認めないからこそ、それをもって送るという行為の道具とみなすことができるのだろう。伝えられることの

A visitor bending over to gaze at my *Stone* is one of ten photographs in an illustrated feature (Fig. 13).

1970.6.7
Okada Takahiko, "Viewer's Seat: In Search of New Language," *Asahi Journal* [J]

My *Stone* is the only illustration to accompany the essay, with a comment, "Stones picked up on a dry riverbed and sent via mail were placed here and there in the museum" (p. 34).

1970.6.14
"Tokyo Biennale and New Experiments," Sunday Mainichi [J]
For example, Horikawa Michio picked 13 stones at a river in Takada, Niigata Prefecture and one by one, in order of the numbers he put on them, sent them via registered mail with an instruction on their placement.

1970.6.20
Young People's Reason to Live: For Once-in-Lifetime Youth, ed. Yomiuri Newspaper Social Desk, pub. Yell Books [J]

My *Stones* project is included under "Why Don't You Join 'Mail Art': Groups That Explore the Value of 'Play'" (pp. 91–99).

1970 summer
Joseph P. Love, "The Tenth Tokyo Biennale of Contemporary Art," *Art International*

My *Stone* is illustrated (p. 70) (Fig. 14).

1970.7
Minemura Toshiaki (annotations of illustrated works), "Why Is This Art? On the Occasion of *10th Tokyo Biennale*," *Bijutsu techō* [J]
When a stone was sent from Horikawa, a postman told its recipient, "You are young, but you have a good hobby." Horikawa gathers stones and sends them to friends in order to dig up the meaning of human acts in the circumstances of mundane life. Because he sees no significance in these stones, he can make them into a tool for his act of sending them. Not the content of his message but the act of communication itself concerns him. Postal mailing is only part of it.

Fig. 13   *The Shinano River Plan: 13*, 1970
『週刊文春』6月1日号「芸術・頭の体操」に掲載された《石》
= *Stone* reproduced in "Art as Brain Gymnastics," *Shūkan Bunshun* (June 1, 1970)

Michio Horikawa. *Nakanomata River Plan 13*, 1970. (All photographs by Elizaburo Hara, by courtesy of Commissioner-General Yusuke Nakahara and the Mainichi Newspapers, sponsors of the 1970 Tokyo Biennale)

Fig. 14   *The Shinano River Plan: 13*, 1970
『アート・インターナショナル』誌 1970年夏号に掲載された《石》 = *Stone* reproduced in *Art International* (summer 1970)

内容ではなく、伝達ということそれ自体が彼の関心事なのである。郵送はそのまた一部分でしかない。

1970.7

大岡信「特集：東京ビエンナーレを告発する」
『芸術新潮』

ただ、あるということの猛烈な事実をどう受けとめているのか。見、感じる行為、認識する行為、行う行為、……沈黙する行為、語り示す行為、……日々、一定の重さの石を河原に拾い、それを主催者に送りとどける行為とは？ そして、その行為をこの石は語らない。見るものはただ通り過ぎる。

私の「石」の作品写真には上のような批判のコメントが添えられた。この大岡信のコメントが一番冷徹に私の作品の不備を指摘していたと受け止めている。私のアポロ13号にちなむメール・アートは解決すべき課題のみを多々残した訳である。この経験から、その後《石》を送る時は切手を貼る宛名の荷札の他に「地球の石 the stone on the earth」や「反戦 anti War」などとプリントした札を付け足すようになっていった。

1970.6

6月に入って東京会場から9個の《石》が荷物として返送されてきた。その石の一番大きな石を記念に残し、8個を採取地で開梱。それらは瞬時にただの石に戻って中ノ俣川の川原に同化していった (Fig. 15.1)。

記念に残した《石》は生家の応接間の本棚に飾っておいた。しかし、生家が改築された際に片付けられて所在不明。

また、別便で、こちらから送付した際の荷札が数枚送られてきたので記録として保管してきた (Fig. 15.2)。

1970.6.17

The Nakanomata River Plan

送付数：1

送付先

　村上善男

村上は精神生理学研究所の送付者リストの一人。本人より依頼があり応えて送る。後日、返礼として送付した《石》と同じ重さ程度の小岩井農場産バターの瓶詰めが送られてきた。

1970.7

Ōoka Makoto, "Special Feature: Indicting *Tokyo Biennale*," *Geijutsu Shinchō* [J]

How does the artist think of the rigorous fact that [a stone] simply exists? Act of seeing and sensing, act of recognizing, act of acting, … act of being silent, act of narrating, … What does it mean to undertake an act of picking up a stone of certain weight every day at a dry riverbed and sending it to the exhibition office every day? These stones do not talk about his act. The viewer simply passes them by.

My *Stone* is illustrated with the above comment. I find this comment by Ōoka most stringently points out the shortcoming of my series. My mail art in conjunction with Apollo 13 leaves nothing but problems to solve. Based on this reckoning, I begin to add tags with such phrases as "the stone on the earth" and "anti-War" printed on them, in addition to mail tags for stamps and addresses.

1970.6

In a package, 9 *Stones* are freighted back from Tokyo's exhibition. Among them, I keep the largest one at home as a record. I bring the rest to the riverbed and remove the wires. They immediately revert back to mere stones and become part of the riverbed of the Nakanomata River (Fig. 15.1).

I place the *Stone* I decided to keep on a bookshelf in the drawing room of my parents' house. However, it goes missing when the house is renovated. Its present whereabouts is unknown.

Separately, the exhibition office sends back a few mail tags I used when I sent *Stones* to the exhibition and I decide to preserve them as records (Fig. 15.2).

1970.6.17

The Nakanomata River Plan
Number of stones sent: 1
Addressees
　Murakami Yoshio

Murakami is on the mailing list of Psychophysiology Research Institute [and came to know of my *Stones* project]. He asks me to send him a *Stone*, and I oblige. Later, he sends me bottles of butter made by Koiwai Farm. The weight of butter approximately equals that of my *Stone* sent to him.

1970.8.12–15

ニルヴァーナ展（京都市美術館）に参加

　前山忠、佐藤秀治と京都旅行をした。ニルヴァーナ展では、5円玉に「あなたに5円あげます」とメッセージを書いた荷札をつけて観客に配布し、また持ち帰れるように展示する作品、《往復葉書によるニルヴァーナ展への投函指示》などを出品。

1970.8.15

6月の人間と物質展京都会場で展示した《石》を保管先から受け取り、三条大橋近くの土堤で針金と荷札を外して鴨川へ返却する。毎日新聞社の峯村敏明にあらかじめお願いして、立ち会っていただく。また友人の竹田潔に写真撮影をお願いする。その後大阪へ、翌日に万国博覧会を半日程度見学する。アメリカ館など長蛇の待ち時間で入れるはずもなく、彫刻のあった広場とキューバの展示館に入ってゲバラのポップ・アートのような大きな顔写真を見たのが記憶にある。

1970.8.29

The Nakanomata River Plan（the stone on the earth）

送付数：1
送付先
　企画展 Situation Concepts（1971年2月開催）に出品

8.18付けで盛岡市在住のVOU会員の高橋昭八郎から展覧会への参加依頼が送られてきたので、オーストリア・インスブルックのギャルリ・イム・タクシスパレスのキュレーター、ピーター・ヴェラーマイヤーに送る。この時から《石》のコンセプトを明確に伝えるため「the stone on the earth」「地球の石」と印刷した札を付け始めた（Fig. 16）。

1970.9 以降

第2期精神生理学研究所の活動として、精神生理学研究所の旗印で、白根山での大きな岩から飛び降りた行為の記録《Mt. Shirane Plan》、切手不足でハガキを送り相手に不足料金を倍払いをさせてしまう《切手不足ハガキ・シリーズ》などゲリラ的メール・アート数例を実践する。これらの作品は送付相手のところに残されているものがあるかもしれない。自分の手元にはほとんどない。

1970.8.12–15

Together with Maeyama and Satō Hideharu, I travel to Kyoto to participate in *Nirvana* at Kyoto Municipal Museum of Art with a few works. One is a multiple that incorporates a real five-yen coin, each accompanied by a tag saying "I am giving you a five-yen coin." I distribute it to visitors and display it so that visitors can take one with them. Another work is *Mailing Instruction for Nirvana Exhibition by a Postcard with a Reply Card Attached*.

1970.8.15

I retrieve my *Stones* shown in June in *Tokyo Biennale 1970: Between Man and Matter* at Kyoto Municipal Museum of Art and kept for me after the exhibition. Near the Sanjō Bridge, I go down to the bank of the Kamo River, remove the wires and tags from the stones, and return them to the river. In advance I made an arrangement with Minemura Toshiaki of the Mainichi newspaper company to witness the act. I also asked my friend Takeda Kiyoshi to photograph it. After the act, I go to Osaka. On the following day, I spend half a day to see Expo '70. There was a long line to enter the American pavilion, so I gave up. I remember seeing a plaza with sculptures and a blown-up Pop Art–like photograph of Che Guevara at the Cuban pavilion.

1970.8.29

The Nakanomata River Plan (the stone on the earth)
Number of stones sent: 1
Addressees
　Sent to *Situation Concepts*

On August 18, Takahashi Shōhachirō in Morioka, a member of the poetry collective VOU, forwarded me a request for participation. I mail a *Stone* to the exhibition curator Peter Weiermair for his exhibition at Galerie im Taxispalais, Innsbruck, Austria to open in February 1971. With this mailing, I introduce a mail tag bearing the phrases "the stone on the earth" and "地球の石" (*chikyū no ishi*) to communicate my concept more clearly (Fig. 16).

1970.9 onward

I personally appropriate the banner of Psychophysiology Research Institute and undertake its "second phase" activities through mail art. Among my guerrilla works are *Mt. Shirane Plan* (which involves the record of jumping down from a huge rock on the mountain) and *Insufficient Postage Postcard Series* (in which recipients

Fig. 15.1   *The Shinano River Plan: 13*, 1970
東京ビエンナーレから返送されてきた《石》を中ノ俣川に返す
= Returning *Stones* sent back from *Tokyo Biennale* to the Nakanomata River

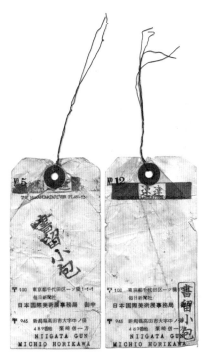

Fig. 15.2   *The Shinano River Plan: 13*, 1970
東京ビエンナーレから返送された《石》の荷札 = Mail tags for *Stone* sent back from *Tokyo Biennale*

Fig. 16   *The Shinano River Plan (the stone on the earth)*, 1970
初の外国展出品の準備。作品コンセプトの「地球の石 = the stone on the earth」を印刷した荷札を付ける
= Preparation for my very first participation in a foreign exhibition;
introducing the first printed mail tag signaling my concept "the stone on the earth"

1970.9.12

ドイツの画商、ポール・マエンツ（Paul Maenz）より手紙をもらい、深く考えずに東京ビエンナーレのカタログを送る。

1970.10.24

The Nakanomata River Plan（the stone on the earth）

送付数：1

送付先

　　ポール・マエンツ

1970.12

「特集：行為する芸術家たち」『美術手帖』

ヨシダヨシエ「単独行為者の超劇場：底知れぬ狂気の営為」

佐藤総理に石を送った新潟の堀川紀夫は、同じ《信濃川プラン》の一環として 69 年 12 月 18* 日の日付で、ホワイト・ハウスのニクソン大統領に九百九十グラムの石を送ったが、この石が送られてゆくコースで起こった不可知のイヴェント、十日町郵便局員、空港関係者、スチュワーデス、ワシントンの郵便配

達夫、ホワイト・ハウスの秘書官などを大雑把におもい浮かべてみても、これに関わった視点やイマジネーションはズタズタである。小説家さながら、それを再構成する余裕もなければ興味もない。（58 頁）

前山忠「存在のギリギリの不可能性としての行為を」

例えばグループ《GUN》のメンバーである堀川紀夫君のように、石や五円玉を郵送とか直接相手に手渡すとかによって、いわゆる受け手としてよりも物と出会う当事者としての行為を相手に取らせてしまう、いわばそこでは創作者と観衆といった両者の二元的関係ではなしに、それぞれが別の事象としての固有な行為者および一回性としてのかけがえのない場として在るわけである。（80 頁）

GUN の《雪のイメージを変えるイベント》の写真などが掲載される。ヨシダの文中（*）で、正しい日付は 69 年 12 月 7 日。

1971.1.31–2.9

アポロ 14 号　月面着陸、船外活動、地球帰還

---

are required to pay twice the balance of insufficient postage to receive it). I have kept few records of these works in my hands, although some recipients may have kept them.

1970.9.12

I receive a letter from Paul Maenz, a German dealer. Without thinking much, I mail him a copy of the Tokyo Biennale catalogue.

1970.10.24

The Nakanomata River Plan (the stone on the earth)

Number of stones sent: 1

Addressees

　　Paul Maenz

1970.12

"Special Feature: Artists Acting Out," *Bijutsu techō*

Yoshida Yoshie, "Ultra-Theater of Solitary Action-Practitioners: Acts of Bottomless Insanity"

Horikawa Michio in Niigata, who sent a stone to Prime Minister Satō, had also sent a 990-gram stone to President Nixon at the White House on December 18*, 1969 as part of his *The Shinano River Plan*. Imagine unknowable events that occurred during

the mailing of this stone, which roughly involved a Tōkamachi postal office clerk, airport personnel, flight attendants, a postman in Washington, D.C., and White House staff. Diverse viewpoints and imaginations were involved and shuttered. I have no time for reconstructing them like a novelist, nor am I interested in doing it (p. 58).

Maeyama Tadashi, "An Act for the Near Impossibility of Being"

For example, Horikawa Michio, a GUN member, makes the recipients undertake not so much the act of receiving a thing but that of encountering it by giving them, say, stones or five-yen coins via postal mail or direct hand delivery. What arises there is not the binary relationship of the creator and the audience, but an irreplaceable one-time site for each actor particular to each event (p. 80).

GUN's *Event to Change the Image of Snow* is reproduced. In Yoshida's text (*), the correct date is December 7, 1969.

1971.1.31–2.9

The Apollo 14 mission encompasses lunar landing,

extravehicular activities on the lunar surface, and
flight home.

1971.3
The Nakanaomata River Plan（the stone on the earth）
送付数：1
送付先
　言葉とイメージ展へ招待出品

針生一郎企画、ピナール画廊（東京）開催のグループ展のために《石》を出品。加えて佐藤栄作総理を扱った《零円切手》第1号を出品。
　《零円切手》は《石》から発想し、郵送に不可欠な切手の型を借用し、本物の切手の日本郵便という文字を反転させてレイアウトした。「切手不足ハガキシリーズ」が先例にある。1967年作の赤瀬川原平の「本物の零円札」は大きなヒント。2001年以後の《Stamp Series》の原型となる。
　この際に《石》の活動について朝日新聞社の取材を受け、会場のピナール画廊で撮影していただく（Figs. 17.1–2）。

1971.4.3
│「石ころ先生」『朝日新聞』社会面

1971.7.26–8.7
アポロ15号 月面着陸、船外活動、地球帰還

1971.8
突然、活動を始めた北川フラムからハガキをもらう。8月下旬ごろに新潟日報の女性記者に会い、「神無月新潟ジャズロックカーニバル」のポスターとチケット制作で協力することになる。

1971.10.21（国際反戦デー）
The Nakanomata River Plan（the stone on the earth）
送付数：4
送付先
　河口龍夫
　斉藤義明
　水上旬
　ヨシダヨシエ

1971–72
《mail art 写真絵葉書》シリーズ（10種類）を制作。勤務校の現像室でハガキサイズに写真を現像。このシリー

1971.3
The Nakanomata River Plan (the stone on the earth)
Number of stones sent: 1
Addressees
　Sent to *Word and Image*

I send a *Stone* to the exhibition curated by the critic Haryū Ichirō at Pinar Gallery in Tokyo.
　With this exhibition, I also inaugurate *Zero-Yen Stamp* series with its first work that satirizes Prime Minister Satō Eisaku. This series is an extension of *Stones*, in that I borrow the format of stamps necessary for postal mailing. I incorporate a mirror image of 日本郵便 (Japan Postal Mail) in design. It followed *Insufficient Postage Postcard Series* and is inspired by Akasegawa Genpei's 1967 work, *Greater Japan Zero-Yen Note*. The series will serve as a prototype for the post-2001 *Stamp Series*.
　In conjunction, I am interviewed by an Asahi reporter on *Stones* and I am photographed with my Stone at Pinar Gallery (Figs. 17.1–2).

1971.4.3
│ "A Stone Teacher," *Asahi shinbun*, social desk [J]

1971.7.26–8.7
The Apollo 15 mission encompasses lunar landing, extravehicular activities on the lunar surface, and flight home.

1971.8
Kitagawa Fram, who has just begun to work in art, sends me a postcard out of the blue. After a meeting with a woman reporter of *Niigata nippō* (Niigata daily) in late August, I agree to produce a poster and ticket design for *Kannazuki Niigata Jazz Rock Carnival*.

1971.10.21 (International Antiwar Day)
The Nakanomata River Plan (the stone on the earth)
Number of stones sent: 4
Addressees
　Kawaguchi Tatsuo
　Saito Yoshiaki
　Mizukami June
　Yoshida Yoshie

Fig. 17.1   *The Nakanomata River Plan (the stone on the earth)*, 1970
引き続き「地球の石」を印刷した荷札を使用
= Continuing to use the printed mail tag of "the stone on the earth"

Fig. 17.2   *The Nakanomata River Plan (the stone on the earth)*, 1970
ピナール画廊での撮影 = Posing with my *Stone* at Pinar Gallery

ズの送付数は少なく、リストは作成しなかった。

1972.4.16–4.27
アポロ 16 号 月面着陸、船外活動、地球帰還

1972.4
『行為に賭ける』『現代の美術 Art Now』第 11 巻 講談社刊
GUN《雪のイメージを変えるイベント》が 86–87 頁
とカバーの裏面に掲載される。

1972.5
「壮烈絵巻・日本芸術界大激戦」『美術手帖』
構成＝赤瀬川原平・松田哲夫　絵＝南伸宏のイラスト
に描かれる。

1972.10
「特集：誌面解放計画」『美術手帖』
田中角栄総理を「日本列島改悪論者像」とキャプショ
ンした《零円切手》で参加。

1972.12.7–19
アポロ 17 号 月面着陸、船外活動、地球帰還

1972.12.13
The Nakanaomata River Plan: 17
送付数：5
送付先
　彦坂尚嘉
　関根哲男（GUN メンバー）
　佐藤秀治（GUN メンバー）
　前山忠（GUN メンバー）
　本人

私の《石を送るメール・アート》はアポロ計画の月の
石採取に「因む」ことで生成し、実行してきた。アポ
ロ 14 号以降も継続してきた。しかし、そのアポロ計
画は 17 号で最後となった。その最後に際し、5 個の《石》
を送った。アポロ計画が終わり、月の石に「因む」意
味は立ち消え、私は《石》の幕を引くことを決断した。

1971–72
I create *Photo Picture Postcard Series*, with 10 different
images. I print photos in postcard size at my school's
darkroom. Not many are mailed and no address list is
made.

1972.4.16–4.27
The Apollo 16 mission encompasses lunar landing,
extravehicular activities on the lunar surface, and
flight home.

1972.4
Art of Action and Concept, *Art Now*, no. 11, pub.
Kōdansha [J]

GUN's *Event to Change the Image of Snow* is illustrated
on pp. 86–87 and the back cover.

1972.5
"Great Battles of the World of Geijutsu in Japan,"
Bijutsu techō [J]

My *Stones* project is included in this illustrated chronicle of contemporary Japanese art conceived by Akasegawa Genpei and Matsuda Tetsuo and illustrated by

Minami Nobuhiro.

1972.10
"Special Feature: A Project of Liberating Magazine
Pages" [J]

I contribute *Zero-Yen Stamp* with Prime Minister
Tanaka Kakuei with a caption "Japanese Archipelago
Malformer."

1972.12.7–19
The Apollo 17 mission encompasses lunar landing,
extravehicular activities on the lunar surface, and
flight home.

1972.12.13
The Nakanomata River Plan: 17
Number of stones sent: 5
Addressees
　Hikosaka Naoyoshi
　Sekine Tetsuo (GUN member)
　Satō Hideharu (GUN member)
　Maeyama Tadashi (GUN member)
　Myself

者会見の言葉を切り取り、《天皇陛下在位51周年記念零円切手》を2種類発行。

1977.10

上越市在住で北川フラムの父である北川省一の『良寛游戯』がアディン書房より出版される。その後も次々と北川の良寛書が出版されるようになる。その良寛話し、良寛論に多くを学ぶ。

1978.9

「図説印刷のフォークロア グラフィズム北の拠点＝盛岡」『デザイン』

ある日、新潟の堀川紀夫から送り届けられた荷物は、その荷姿の簡潔さにおいて、前代未聞のものであった。それはものとしての内容物と、「荷札」の機能がストレートに結ばれていて、「荷札」がものと対等に構造そのものがまるごと露出しているのだった。

この記事を監修した村上善男に1970年6月17日付けで送った《石》がイラストで紹介される。

1980年代

雪の上に自らの体を投げ出してその形を写真に収める《Snow Performance》シリーズを発見、その後10年近くの間展開を続ける。

1982

雑誌『太陽』で《田中角栄零円切手》が掲載中止に至った事例が起きる。田中切手には「日本列島改悪論者」のキャプションが記されている。

1985.5

The Shinano River Plan '85

送付数：4

送付先

　環境としてのイメージ展へ招待出品（2個）

　大久保淳二

　駒野直

1972年のアポロ17号に因んで友人の関根哲男に送った《石》を当時高校生であった山崎均が見た。その縁で山崎が学芸員を務める兵庫県立近代美術館で1985

Asahi (Weekly Asahi), but the idea is rejected at the final stage due to concern over its satirical nature.

1977.1

Horikawa Michio, "How *My Zero-Yen Stamp Commemorating the Lockheed Scandal* Was Not Reproduced," *Shin Nihon bungaku=Nova japana literaturo* [J]

1977.9

I issue two kinds of *Zero-Yen Commemorative Stamp for the 51st Anniversary of Emperor Shōwa's Reign*, which incorporate news reports on the emperor's visit in the U.S. in 1975 and his words from his first ever news conference upon his return.

1977.10

A Jōetsu resident and father of Kitagawa Fram, Kitagawa Seiichi publishes *Ryōkan yūgi* (Ryōkan plays) from Adin Shobō, followed by a number of books on the Edo monk Ryōkan by him, I learn much from Kitagawa's study of Ryōkan.

1978.9

"Folklore of Print, Illustrated: A Northern Base of Graphism, Morioka," *Dezain: A Bimonthly Review of Design* [J]

One day, I received a package from Horikawa Michio, a friend of mine in Niigata. It was unprecedented in terms of the simplicity of its packaging. The content (object) of the package and the role of the mailing tag were functionally linked in a straightforward manner. The tag asserts an equal presence to the object, with its functionality completely made visible.

Murakami Yoshio, who edits this article, illustrates my *Stone* sent to him on June 17, 1970.

1980s

I develop the series *Snow Performance*, in which I throw my body onto the snow and photograph the imprint. I continue the series for close to the next ten years.

1982

A plan to reproduce my *Zero-Yen Stamp (Tanaka Kakuei)* in the monthly *Taiyō = The Sun* is canceled. The stamp carries the caption "Japanese Archipelago Malformer."

年 10 月に開催される「環境としてのイメージ」展に招待を受けた。上越教育大学大学院に研修派遣中のこと。東京造形大学で成田克彦助教授に学んだ 1 年後輩の駒野直を同道して、13 年ぶりに信濃川へ出かけ十日町橋の西側で石を拾う。

美術館にはゴツゴツした黒の石と丸みのある灰色系の石の 2 個を送る（Figs. 18.1–2）。駒野と 1969 年の《The Shinano River Plan: 12》で一緒に石を拾ってくれた教え子の大久保淳二にも送る。

1986.2
代官山ヒルサイドギャラリー（北川フラム主宰）にて《Snow Performance》シリーズで個展。

1986.9.7
「芸術的自由人」TNN テレビ新潟に出演。

1987.9
「TNN にいがた美術散歩 PART-1 新潟の作家」
TNN 発行（46–47、126 頁）

1989 以降
アクリル絵画を断続的に展開。《Heisei》《天象》《Edge》《Cosmic》などをタイトルにしてきている。

1993.4
「瀧口修造のオブジェ・コレクション全 250」『太陽』《石》が掲載される（75 頁）。

1993.7.15
『Snow Performance』自家出版
一念発起し作品集を出版。中原佑介にコメントを書いていただくが、テキストの英訳に手間取る。最終的には当時勤務していた松代中学校の ALT でオーストラリア・タスマニア島出身のフラン・マクマーレンの監修を受ける。アートフロントギャラリーの力を借りて全国的に配布。

1994.8.1–11
Ginza Gallery House でアクリルによるレリーフ的絵画で個展。
パンフレット：藤島俊会「絵画の視覚と現実の視覚」

1985.5
The Shinano River Plan '85
Number of stones sent: 4
Addressees
Sent to *Image as Environment* (2 stones)
Ōkubo Junji
Komano Sunao

In 1972, I sent a *Stone* to my friend Sekine Tetsuo in conjunction with the Apollo 17 mission. Yamazaki Hitoshi, who saw it as a high schooler, is instrumental in inviting me to show in the exhibition at Hyōgo Prefectural Museum of Modern Art, Kobe, where he now works as a curator.

I receive the invitation to the exhibition while attending a workshop for teachers at the graduate school of Jōetsu University of Education. After 13 years, I for the first time return to the Shinano River and pick stones on the river's western side. I am accompanied by Komano Sunao, my junior colleague by one year, who studied at Tokyo Zōkei University in Tokyo under Narita Katsuhiko.

I send 2 *Stones* to the museum, one gray and round and the other black and rough in shape (Figs. 18.1–2). I also send 1 *Stone* each to Komano and Ōkubo Junji, another student of mine, who both gathered stones with me for *The Shinano River Plan: 12.*

1986.2
I have a solo exhibition with the series *Snow Performances* at Daikanyam Hillside Gallery (directed by Kitagawa Fram) in Tokyo.

1986.9.7
I appear in "Artistic Free People," a program on TNN (Niigata Television).

1987.9
TNN Niigata Art Walk: Part 1 (Artists in Niigata), pub. TNN (pp. 46–47, 126) [J]

1989 onward
I intermittently explore creating paintings in acrylic, with such titles as *Heisei*, *Tenshō* (Heavenly phenomena), *Edge*, and *Cosmic*.

1993.4
"Takiguchi Shūzō's 250 *Objets* Collections," *Taiyō* = *The Sun* [J]

Fig. 18.1   *The Shinano River Plan '85*, 1985
兵庫県立近代美術館に送った灰色の《石》
= A gray *Stone* sent to Hyōgo Prefectural Museum of Modern Art, Kobe

Fig. 18.2   *The Shinano River Plan '85*, 1985
兵庫県立近代美術館に送った黒色の《石》
= A black *Stone* sent to Hyōgo Prefectural Museum of Modern Art, Kobe

1994.10.10–30
富山市の紡績工場跡地の舞台芸術パークを会場とする Art Edge '94 展へ招待。コミッショナーは初瀬部真一。「深化する近代の意識」の表題に平面に差異を作り出すレリーフ的絵画シリーズを出品。

この後、《Edge》というタイトル名を用いてレリーフ的絵画を展開し、またアルミ、ブリキの腐食による版画に挑戦。そして飯室哲也、稲憲一郎と共同参画で版画集『汎』を出版。それに伴って銀座と甲府で開催されたグループ展にも数回参加する。

1996.1
NHK 番組「人間マップ：先生は雪のアーチスト」に出演。全国放映される。《Snow Performance》の制作プロセスが放映される。番組内で《石》も紹介される。

1997.2.16
『汎』第 1 集 飯室哲也、稲憲一郎、堀川紀夫による版画集（60 部）

1997.10
「HIKOSAKA'S LONG INTERVIEW 拳銃（GUN）と〈石〉と〈切手〉：『人間と物質』展作家・堀川紀夫」『ACRYLART アクリラート』32 号
現代美術のアーティストが地元の石を芸術として発信したというのは、レイシーの 1984 年と比較しても堀川さんの 1969 年という早さと、模倣ではないオリジナリティを含めて、今日的なパブリック・アートに先駆けるものとして私は高く評価したいです（9 頁）。
彦坂尚嘉が詳細なインタビューをもとにしてまとめた記事。《石》、新潟現代美術家集団 GUN の活動などが再評価される。この対談のまとめに関するやり取りをメールで行う。

1998.5
堀川紀夫「私の良寛さん」『LR 7』

1999.4.5–16
眼の座標 X ―― それぞれの地平展（飯室哲也、稲憲一郎との 3 人展、代々木アートギャラリーにて）

My *Stone* sent to Takiguchi Shūzō is reproduced (p. 75).

1993.7.15
Snow Performance, self-published [J]

I self-publish to give an overview of the series. I ask Nakahara Yūsuke to write a comment. It takes some time to have it translated into English. The final version is edited by Fran McFarlan [spelling unknown], from Tasmania, who was an Assistant Language Teacher at Matsudai Middle School, where I teach at the time. The volume is distributed nationwide with assistance by Art Front Gallery in Tokyo.

1994.8.1–11
I have a solo exhibition at Ginza Gallery House with a series of relief paintings executed in acrylic.

Brochure: Fujishima Toshie, "Sight of Painting, Sight of Reality" [J]

1994.10.10–30
I am invited to show at *Art Edge '94*, held at a "stage art park" created on the former site of a spinning mill in Toyama, under the commissionership of Hasebe Shin'ichi. I presented a series of painting reliefs, titled *Deepening Modern Consciousness*, that generate sight differences on surfaces.

Thereafter, under the title *Edge*, I develop a series of painting reliefs. I also work in printmaking by corroding aluminum and tinplate. I collaborate with Iimuro Tetsuya and Ina Ken'ichirō to publish a book of prints, *Han*. In conjunction, I participate in several group exhibitions in Ginza, Tokyo, and Kōfu.

1996.1
I appear in NHK's program *Human Map: Teacher Is a Snow Artist*, which is broadcast nationwide. It features the production process of *Snow Performance*. *Stones* are also shown.

1997.2.16
Han: Volume 1, a book of prints by Iimuro Tetsuya, Ina Ken'ichirō, and Horikawa Michio (edition of 60) [J]

1997.10
"Hikosaka's Long Interview: Horikawa Michio of GUN, Stones, Stamps, *Tokyo Biennale*," *Acrylart*,

『新潟現代美術家集団 GUN と私』自作資料
3 人展を機会に GUN での活動を振り返る。

1999.11.9–21
堀川紀夫展 見附市今井美術館ギャラリー
| パンフレット：八木宏昌「『絵画』へ」

1999.12
ロンドンのテート・モダンの開館記念センチュリー・シティ展東京セクションのキュレーターを務める富井玲子が『アクリラート』32 号のインタビュー記事を見て、堀川宅を来訪。《石を送るメール・アート》とその関係資料を調査し評価。同展へ招待される。この出品の機会に同作品の意味が全く色褪せていないことを改めて認識して、再開を決意。以後、石を送る意味を見つけて継続実践してきている。

2000.2
三条市月岡小学校に校長として勤務。卒業学年の記念植樹として宮島達男の柿の木プロジェクトに参加。長崎被爆柿の子孫を 2 本植樹させていただいた。

2000.7.17
| 堀川紀夫「大地の芸術祭を前に 田園、へき地のフレームに新たな美術の開発を試みる」『新潟日報』（投稿掲載）

2000.7.20–9.10
第 1 回大地の芸術祭に参加。北川フラムをディレクターとして越後妻有地域で開催された芸術祭の松代ギャラリーロードに、《アートトリエンナーレのためのベンチ》を出品。

同芸術祭にアルフレッド・ジャーは、《小さな美術館》プロジェクトで参加。そのジャーのプロジェクトに地元キュレーター宮崎俊英（当時松代中学校教頭）が協働し、GUN の《雪のイメージを変えるイベント》を展示作品に選出。その制作に予算が付いて、羽永光利より譲り受けていたポジフィルムを大きく拡大して展示することができた。

その写真は、その後東京都現代美術館に寄贈。2008 年の新潟現代美術家集団 GUN の軌跡展（ギャラリー mu-an とスペース・トキ）ではそれを借りて展示。2012 年に新潟県立近代美術館で開催の GUN──新潟に前衛

---

no. 32 [J]
You as a contemporary artist used local stones as art to communicate in 1969. It was way earlier, for example, than Suzanne Lacey's 1984 work [such as *Whisper, the Waves, the Wind*]. Moreover, it was no imitation, it was original, and it anticipated today's public art. I accordingly give a high mark to it (p. 9).

An article based on Hikosaka Naoyoshi's detailed interview with me, in which he newly evaluated GUN: Niigata Contemporary Artists Collective and *Mail Art by Sending Stones*. We exchanged e-mails during the editing process.

1998.5
| Horikawa Michio, "My Ryōkan," *LR 7* [J]

1999.4.5–16
I show in *Eye's Axis X: Individual Horizons*, a three-person exhibition (with Iimuro Tetsuya and Ina Ken'ichirō) at Yoyogi Art Gallery in Tokyo

| *GUN: Niigata Contemporary Artists Collective and I*, self-published [J]

On the occasion of the exhibition, I reflect on my activities with GUN.

1999.11.9–21
I have a solo exhibition at Imai Museum Gallery, Mitsuke.

| Brochure: Yagi Hiromasa, "Toward 'Painting'" [J]

1999.12
Reiko Tomii, who saw my interview in *Acrylart*, no. 32, visits me at my house in preparation for her Tokyo section for Tate Modern's inaugural exhibition *Century City*. She studies the material related to *Mail Art by Sending Stones*, and decides to invite me to her section. Upon her invitation, I come to realize that the meaning of the series has not faded at all. Thereafter, I continue to send *Stones* with this reckoning.

2000.2
At Tsukioka Elementary School, where I am Headmaster, the graduating class participates in Miyajima Tatsuo's *Kaki Tree Project* by planting two persimmon trees descended from a tree irradiated in Nagasaki.

美術があった頃展でも同様に展示。

2000.8.10
「海を渡る石のモダンアート 英・国際美術展へ出品へ」『新潟日報』

2000.7.29–8.20
見えない境界 変貌するアジアの美術 光州ビエンナーレ 2000（アジア・セクション）新潟アジア文化祭へ招待。《Snow Performance Series》を出品。コミッショナーは谷新。

2000.12.8
The Shinano River Plan 2000
送付数：3
送付先
　センチュリー・シティ展に出品
　富井玲子
　本人

出品の《石》は、開催館のテート・モダンを統括する

テート・ギャラリーの館長ニコラス・セロタ卿に送った。12月8日は英国も巻き込んだ日米開戦へつながった真珠湾攻撃メモリアルの日。

2001.1.1
The Shinano River Plan 2001
送付数：1
送付先
　センチュリー・シティ展に出品

テート・ギャラリー館長ニコラス・セロタ卿に21世紀の初日の1月1日に世界平和への願いを込めて送った（Fig. 19）。

2001.2.1–4.29
センチュリー・シティ展（テート・モダン、ロンドン）
　館長にあてた新しい石2個にくわえて、旧作の石4個（送付先：本人、前山忠、瀧口修造、山本孝）が東京セクションに展示された（Fig. 20）。
　展示終了後、富井玲子の尽力により Tate 宛の《石》2個はテート・ギャラリーのアーカイブに収蔵された。

2000.7.17
Horikawa Michio, "In Advance of Echigo-Tsumari Triennial: Exploring a New Framework of Art in Remote Areas," *Niigata nippō* (unsolicited contribution) [J]

2000.7.20–9.10
I participate in the first Echigo-Tsumari Triennial, directed by Kitagawa Fram. I present *Bench for Art Triennial* at Matsudai Gallery Road.

I also participate in *Bunka no Hako*, a project by Alfredo Jaar, who collaborates with Miyazaki Toshihide, a local curator and then vice principal of Matsudai Middle School. They select GUN's *Event to Change the Image of Snow* to show in their project. Its budget makes it possible for me to create a large color print of the work from a color positive entrusted to me from Hanaga Mitsutoshi.

I subsequently donate the print to Museum of Contemporary Art, Tokyo. When we organize *Trajectory of GUN: Niigata Contemporary Artists Collective* at Gallery mu-an, Nagaoka, and Toki Art Space, Tokyo in 2008–9, we borrow it from the museum; we also borrow it for *GUN: When There Was Avant-Garde Art in Niigata* at Niigata Prefectural Museum of Modern Art in 2012.

2000.8.10
"Modern Artwork of Stones Crossing the Sea: To Be Exhibited at an International Exhibition in the U.K.," *Niigata nippō* [J]

2000.7.29–8.20
I am invited to *Invisible Boundary: Metamorphosed Asian Art—Asian Section of Gwangju Biennale 2000*, under the commissionership of Tani Arata. I present *Snow Performance Series*.

2000.12.8
The Shinano River Plan 2000
Number of stones sent: 3
Addressees
　Sent to *Century City*
　Reiko Tomii
　Myself

I sent a *Stone* for the exhibition to Sir Nicholas Serota, director of Tate Gallery in London, of which the exhibition venue Tate Modern is part. I select the date of mailing, December 8, to commemorate the Pearl Harbor Attack that triggered the war between Japan and the U.S., which also involved the U.K.

同展の出品者松沢宥、彦坂尚嘉、東京画廊山本豊津、田畑幸人、友人の小川文雄、堀川紀幸（長男）の７名でロンドンへ旅行。オープニングに出席。またロンドン観光と美術館研修をする。

2001.2.2
ロンドンのタイ料理店にて松沢宥の79歳誕生日を祝う夕食会が行われる。富井夫妻と小川、彦坂、堀川親子が参加。

センチュリー・シティ展関連出版物 ——————

2001.2.1
富井玲子「挑発された思想：1970年頃の東京十景（1967–73）」『センチュリー・シティ』展カタログ（214–215頁）[E]

2001.2.1
『ザ・オブザーバー紙によるセンチュリー・シティ展ガイド』（18–19頁）[E]

2001.1.22
「新潟ひと模様：拾い集め郵送した石 20世紀象徴の作品に」『読売新聞』新潟版

2001.2.9
「石に刻んだ20世紀 メール・アート 英で注目」『新潟日報』

2001.2.26
The Shinano River Plan
送付数：1
送付先
　新潟市のアトリエ我廊での個展に出品

21世紀を迎えての回顧展形式の個展に出品するため、画廊主・藤由暁男宛に送る。

2001.2.27–3.4
堀川紀夫個展「新世紀に向けて・いわゆる一つの小さな回顧として」（アトリエ我廊、新潟市）

2001.1.1
The Shinano River Plan 2001
Number of stones sent: 1
Addressees
　Sent to Century City

I send a *Stone* to Sir Nicholas Serota, director of Tate Gallery, with a hope for world peace on the first day of the 21st century (Fig. 19).

2001.2.1–4.29
My participation in *Century City* at Tate Modern includes 2 *Stones* sent to the museum, along with 4 old *Stones* (sent to myself, Maeyama Tadashi, Takiguchi Shūzō, and Yamamoto Takashi), in the Tokyo section (Fig. 20).

　After the exhibition, Reiko Tomii is instrumental in helping me to donate the 2 *Stones* I sent the museum to its archive. The *Stone* sent to Tomii is donated to the Getty Research Institute in Los Angeles in June 2003.

　I join a group tour to London organized by two participating artists (Matsuzawa Yutaka and Hikosaka Naoyoshi), along with Yamamoto Hozu and Tabata Yukihito of Tokyo Gallery, my friend Ogawa Fumio, and my son Horikawa Michiyuki. I attend the opening and see art and tourist sights.

　On February 2, I join a dinner at a Thai restaurant in London to celebrate the 79th birthday of Matsuzawa Yutaka, with Tomii and her husband, Hikosaka, and my son.

Publications Related to *Century City* ——————

2001.2.1
Reiko Tomii, "Thought Provoked: Ten Views of Tokyo, Circa 1970 (1967–73)," *Century City*, exh. cat. (pp. 214–15)

2001.2.1
The Observer Century City Exhibition Guide (pp. 18–19)

2001.1.22
"Niigata Profiles: Stones Gathered and Mailed Are a Symbol of the 20th Century," *Yomiuri shinbun*, Niigata edition [J]

2001.2.9
"20th Century Carved into Stone: Mail Art Given Attention in the U.K.," *Niigata nippō* [J]

Fig. 19   *The Shinano River Plan 2001*, 2001
テート・ギャラリー館長ニコラス・セロタ卿に送った《石》
= *Stone* sent to Sir Nicholas Serota, director of Tate Gallery

Fig. 20   *The Shinano River Plan '85*, 1985
センチュリー・シティ展での《石》6個の展示風景 = 6 *Stones* on view at *Century City* (Tate Modern)

2001.2.28
NHK テレビ「ゆうどき新潟 街スタトーク」に出演。

2001.3
長女堀川美紀、次女堀川絵美がセンチュリー・シティ展を見に英国へ旅行。

2001.7.5–7.25
瀧口修造――夢の漂流物展（富山県民会館美術館）で瀧口修造に送った《石》が展示される。

2001.9.11
米国で同時多発テロ勃発。同時多発テロに触発されて、Photo Shop を使ったデジタル・アート《Stamp Series》を開始する。

2002.2.1
「雪戯四景 おとなたちの雪あそび」『新潟発 季刊 2002』No.004 冬号

2002.5–6
彦坂尚嘉主宰の SNS teoria-kitaibunshi で《Stamp Series》を 30 点程度発表させていただく。

2002.12.15
富井玲子「Circa1970 解題＝テート・モダン『センチュリー・シティ』展東京セクション〈七〉」（連載最終回）『テオリア』28 号（18–19 頁）

［訂正加筆して 2012 年に『現代美術の地平に石を探る 堀川紀夫の《石のメール・アート》』として出版］

2003.5.2
富井玲子よりメールが来る。「LOS の Getty Center で 1970 年に堀川がドイツに送った東京ビエンナーレのカタログを発見した」。このカタログは、マエンツから寄贈されたマエンツ文書アーカイブの一部としてロサンゼルスのゲッティ研究所に収蔵されていたのだ。《石》と同じ手法で郵送された同カタログは「作品」であるという富井のアドバイスを受けて、ゲッティでは、このカタログを一般図書から特別コレクションに分類しなおした。同年 7 月に、このことに関する手紙等の記

2001.2.26
The Shinano River Plan
Number of stones sent: 1
Addressees
　　　Sent to Atelier Garō in Niigata

I send a *Stone* in care of Fujiyoshi Akio, the gallery owner, so that I could include it in my retrospective that marked the beginning of the 21st century.

2001.2.27–3.4
I have a solo exhibition *Toward a New Century: A Small Retrospective*, Atelier Garō, in Niigata.

2001.2.28
I appear in "Evening Niigata: City Station Talk," an NHK program.

2001.3
My two daughters, Horikawa Miki and Emi, travel to the U.K. to see *Century City*.

2001.7.5-7.25
My *Stone* sent to Takiguchi Shūzō is shown in *Takiguchi Shūzō: Drifting Objects of Dreams* at Toyama Kenmin Kaikan Museum.

2001.9.11
September 11 attacks occur in the U.S. Inspired by the incident, I begin the Photoshop-based *Stamp Series* as digital art.

2001 onward
I create *E-Stamps Series* with Photoshop, when occasions arise, and present new works on social media.

2002.2.1
"Four Snow Plays: Snow Play by Adults," *Niigata hatsu kikan 2002* (Quarterly from Niigata 2002), no. 4, Winter [J]

2002.5–6
I present some 30 works of *Stamp Series* at Hikosaka Naoyoshi's social media group, teoria-kitaibunshi.

2002.12.15
Reiko Tomii, "Circa 1970: Tokyo Section of Century City at Tate Modern, 7," Theoria, no. 28 (pp. 18–19) [J]

[An expanded and revised version is published as *Exploring*

録をゲッティに寄贈した。

2003.11
堀川紀夫「Getty での発見物語」『上越芸術彙報』（上越芸術総合研究所）2 号（10–16 頁）
富井玲子のメールを受けてカタログを送った経緯や《石》について書く。

2003.11.9
ゲッティ研究所での企画展のことでチャールズ・メリウェザーが拙宅に取材訪問。

2003
| クリス・アバニ『ダフネの運』レッド・ヘン・プレス刊 [E]

2005.1
| 『E-Mail Stamps Series』自費出版
自作パンフを発行し、「Digital Works "E-Mail Stamps" Series について」を執筆。

2005.2
| 椹木野衣『戦争と万博』美術出版社刊
第 6 章に《石を送るメール・アート》の写真が掲載される（193 頁）。その註 82（316 頁）で「60 年代後半に展開された『石』をめぐる一連のムーブメントの中で、新たに捉え直す必要を感じる」との言葉をいただく。

2005.8.27
|「新たな感性へ挑戦 ギャラリー開設」『上越よみうり』

2005.9.11
The Shinano River Plan 2005.9.11
送付数：1
送付先
　　東京府美術館の時代展へ出品

開催館の東京都現代美術館館長あてに郵送（Fig. 21）。この作品を展覧会終了後に同館へ寄贈。

2005.10.20
|「話題作を再制作 東京都現代美術館に展示」

Stones on the Horizon of Contemporary Art: Horikawa Michio's Mail Art by Sending Stones in 2012.]

2003.5.2
Reiko Tomii e-mails me: "I discovered a copy of *Tokyo Biennale 1970* catalogue, which you sent to Germany in 1970 at Getty Center in Los Angeles." The catalogue sent to Maenz is part of Paul Maenz Archive at the Getty Research Institute (GRI). Upon Tomii's advice that the copy mailed to Germany in a method similar to *Stones* (i.e., no paper wrapping) is a "work of art" by the artist, GRI transfers this copy from its general library section to its special collection. In July 2003, I donate the Maenz-related correspondences and materials to GRI.

2003.11
Horikawa Michio, "A Discovery Story at Getty," *Jōetsu geijutsu ihō*, no. 2 (pp. 10–16) [J]

I write on my mailing of the catalogue and *Mail Art by Sending Stones* after I received Reiko Tomii's e-mail.

2003.11.9
Charles Merewether visits me at home during his research for his exhibition at the Getty Research Institute.

2003
| Chris Abani, *Daphne's Lot*, pub. Red Hen Press (p. 33)

2005.1
| *E-Mail Stamps Series*, self-published [J]

A booklet includes my text, "On Digital Works E-Mail Stamps Series."

2005.2
| Sawaragi Noi, *Sensō to banpaku/World Wars and World Fairs*, pub. Bijutsu Shuppan-sha [J]

In Chapter 6, *Mail Art by Sending Stones* is illustrated (p. 193) and in note 82 (p. 316), Sawaragi writes, "I feel the need to reexamine this work in a movement related to stones in the latter half of the 1960s."

2005.8.27
| "Challenge for a New Sensibility: A Gallery Opened," *Jōetsu Yomiuri* [J]

『上越タイムス』

2005.11.5
「平和祈る石のアート、再評価 ──『東京府美術館の時代展』への出品について」『朝日新聞』新潟県版

2005.12.1
「平和祈り 時代に一石 東京都現代美術館 米テロテーマ再展示」『新潟日報』上越版

2006.4.6
「堀川紀夫展 切手形式で社会描写（ギャラリー檜）」『新潟日報』

2006.8
ブルー・スカイ・プロジェクト国際平和美術展を企画・主催。2006年より2010年まで5回開催。

2006
文化庁メディア芸術祭「日本のメディア芸術100選」アート部門1960年代に《石を送るメール・アート》がノミネートされる。アート部門の1位は岡本太郎の《太陽の塔》が受賞。

2007
富井玲子「『日常性への下降』以後：日本のコレクティビズム、ハイレッド・センターからザ・プレイまで1964–1973年」『モダニズム以後の集団』ミネソタ大学出版会刊 [E]

「彦坂尚嘉インタビュー」聞き手・坂上しのぶ『彦坂尚嘉3つのイベント：現代美術のノワール』ギャラリー16刊（8–9頁）

2007.3
芸術・反芸術・非芸術：戦後日本の公共圏における実験1950–1970年展（ゲッティ研究所、ロサンゼルス）に館蔵品から出品。

テート・モダンのセンチュリー・シティ展に関連して1999年12月8日付でキュレター富井玲子に送った《石》をその後富井がゲッティ研究所へ寄贈（Fig. 22.2）。その《石》の作品、第1回精神生理学研究所の拙作（二

2005.9.11
The Shinano River Plan 2005.9.11
Number of stones sent: 1
Addressees
    Sent to *Age of "Tokyo Metropolitan Art Gallery"*

I send a *Stone* in care of the director of Museum of Contemporary Art, Tokyo, which organizes the exhibition (Fig. 21). I subsequently donate the *Stone* to the museum.

2005.10.20
"Remaking a Highly Publicized Work: Exhibited at Museum of Contemporary Art, Tokyo," *Jōetsu Times* [J]

2005.11.5
"Reevaluation of Stone Art for Peace: On Participation in *Age of 'Tokyo Metropolitan Art Gallery'* Exhibition," *Asahi shinbun*, Niigata edition [J]

2005.12.1
"Throwing a Stone at the Era in Prayer for Peace: Exhibition at Museum of Contemporary Art, Tokyo with the Theme of 9/11 Attacks," *Niigata nippō*, Jōetsu edition [J]

2006.4.6
"Horikawa Michio Exhibition: Portraying Society with Stamps (Gallery Hinoki)," *Niigata nippō* [J]

2006.8
I curate and organize *Blue Sky Project: International Peace Art Exhibition*. The exhibition is held five times from 2006 to 2010.

2006
Mail Art by Sending Stones is nominated for the 1960s Art section of *Japan's Media Art 100 Works* at the Agency for Cultural Affair's Media Art Festival. The first place is given to Okamoto Tarō's *Tower of the Sun*.

2007
Reiko Tomii, "After the Descent to the Everyday: Japanese Collectivism from Hi Red Center to The Play, 1964–1973," *Collectivism after Modernism*, pub. Minneapolis: University of Minnesota Press

2007
"Interview with Hikosaka Naoyoshi by Sakagami Shinobu," *Three Pieces of Naoyoshi Hikosaka*, pub. galerie 16 (pp. 8–9) [J]

クソン大統領に送った《石》の荷姿写真とレシート）、ドイツの
ポール・マエンツに送った東京ビエンナーレ展カタロ
グが展示される（Fig. 22.1）。
　サンフランシスコとロサンゼルスのパック旅行で
ゲッティを訪問。

｜　カタログに図版掲載（108、110 頁）[E]

2008.1.8
The Shinano River Plan 2008
送付数：1
送付先
　新潟現代美術家集団 GUN の軌跡展へ出品

会場のギャラリー mu-an の画廊主の立見迪子に送る。
展覧会後、立見より堀川に返還され作家の個人蔵となる。

2008.1.11
「長岡で『GUN の軌跡』展　前衛開花　生々しく生き
続けるスピリット」『新潟日報』

2008.1.13–27
「新潟現代美術家集団 GUN の軌跡」展（長岡市ギャラリー
mu-an）

2008.1.8
The Shinano River Plan 2008.1.15
送付数：1
送付先
　伏見修

2007 年秋に香川県ソフトマシーン美術館を訪問した際
にお世話になった。

2008.3.31
『**GUN 新潟現代美術家集団 GUN の軌跡 1967–
1975**』自費出版（発行 前山忠＋堀川紀夫）
富井玲子「GUN を世界に着地させる試み：GUN's
Event to Change the Image of Snow」を収録。

2008.4.17–26
堀川紀夫展（スペース 23℃、世田谷区等々力）

2007.3
*Art, Anti-Art, Non-Art: Experimentations in the Public
Sphere in Postwar Japan 1950–1970* at Getty Research
Institute (GRI) in Los Angeles includes three works
from its collections.
　I sent a *Stone* to Reiko Tomii in conjunction with
Tate Modern's *Century City*, and she subsequently
donated it to GRI (Fig. 22.2). Together with it, I find a
sheet from the portfolio Psychophysiology Research
Institute (showing the *Stone* sent to President Nixon
and the post office receipt), and a *Tokyo Biennale 1970*
catalogue I sent to Paul Maenz (Fig. 22.1). I attend the
symposium and visit San Francisco and Los Angeles.

｜　Illustrated on pp. 108, 110 in the catalogue

2008.1.8
The Shinano River Plan 2008
Number of stones sent: 1
Addressees
　**Sent to *Trajectory of GUN: Niigata Contemporary
　Artists Collective***

I send a *Stone* to Tachimi Yūko, the owner of Gallery
mu-an, the exhibition venue. After the exhibition, it is
returned to me and becomes part of the artist's collection.

2008.1.11
｜　"*Trajectory of GUN* Exhibition in Nagaoka: Vivid
｜　and Enduring Flowering of the Vanguard Spirit,"
｜　*Niigata nippō* [J]

2008.1.13–27
*Trajectory of GUN: Niigata Contemporary Artists Collec-
tive* is held at Gallery mu-an in Nagaoka.

2008.1.8
The Shinano River Plan 2008.1.15
Number of stones sent: 1
Addressees
　Fushimi Osamu

In the fall of 2007, I met with him at his Soft Machine
Museum in Kagawa Prefecture. I send a *Stone* to thank
him for his hospitality.

2008.3.31
｜　*GUN: Trajectory of GUN: Niigata Contemporary Artists
｜　Collective 1967–1975* (self-published by Maeyama

Fig. 21   *The Shinano River Plan 2005.9.11*, 2005
東京府美術館の時代 1926〜1970 展に送った《石》
= *Stone* sent to *Age of " Tokyo Metropolitan Art Gallery"* (Museum of Contemporary Art, Tokyo)

Fig. 22.1　芸術・反芸術・非芸術展の展示風景：第1回精神生理学研究所の《石》（上左角）、ポール・マエンツに送った東京ビエンナーレ展カタログ（中央上）、富井玲子に送った《石》（中央下）
= Horikawa at *Art, Anti-Art, Non-Art* (Getty Research Institute), with *Stone* sent to Reiko Tomii (bottom center), a copy of *Tokyo Biennale* catalogue sent to Paul Maenz (top center), and data card of *Stone* sent to Nixon (far left upper corner)

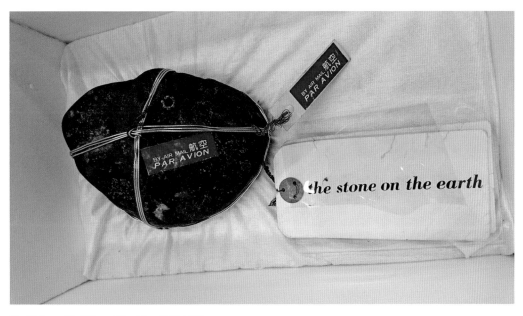

Fig. 22.2　*The Shinano River Plan 2000*, 2000
ゲッティ研究所に寄贈された富井玲子宛の《石》 = *Stone* sent to Sir Nicholas Serota, director of Tate Gallery

『新潟現代美術家集団 GUN と私 (現代美術自分史)』
展覧会を機会に、堀川紀夫自作資料限定 30 部出版。

2008.5.13
「美ここから」『信濃毎日新聞』

2008.6.12
堀川紀夫「『GUN の軌跡 1967–1975』出版：熱く無垢な思い貫く 前衛目指した活動を総括」
『新潟日報』に執筆掲載

2008.8.28
The Shinano River Plan 1969/2008
送付数：1
送付先
ダダカン米寿記念鬼放展に出品

上原誠一郎の企画・出品依頼を受け、ダダカン糸井貫二へのオマージュとして送る。

2008.9.23–12.14
オン・ロケーション展 (セインズベリ視覚芸術センター、英国ノーウィッチ)
テート・ギャラリー・アーカイブ収蔵の《石》2 点が展示される (Fig. 23)。夫婦でイギリス・フランスを旅行し Norwich を訪問する。

展覧会カタログ：『オン・ロケーション：ロバート・スミッソンと同時代作家たちを位置付ける』(126 頁) [E]

2008.10.29
http://www.guardian.co.uk/artanddesign/2008/oct/29/1000-artworks-to-see-before-you-die-art [E]
英『ガーディアン』紙の企画「死ぬ前に見ておくべき美術作品 1000 点」にゲッティの《石》が取り上げられる。

2008 以降
大地の芸術祭の里の「雪アート」が始まる。中里、松代地区の有志と協働して《山ぞりプロジェクト》を連続開催してきている。

Tadashi and Horikawa Michio) [J]

The book includes Reiko Tomii, "An Attempt to Land GUN in World Art History: GUN's *Event to Change the Image of Snow*." [J]

2008.4.17–26
Horikawa Michio Solo Exhibition, Todoroki Space 23°C, Tokyo

On the occasion of the exhibition, I self-publish my personal view of GUN.

GUN: Niigata Contemporary Artists Collective and I (My History of Contemporary Art) (edition of 30) [J]

2008.5.13
"Beauty from Here," *Shinano Mainichi shinbun* [J]

2008.6.12
Horikawa Michio, "The Publication of *Trajectory of Niigata Contemporary Artists Collective GUN 1967–1975*: Having Maintained Innocent Passion—Reflections on Vanguard Activities," *Niigata nippō* [J]

2008.8.28
The Shinano River Plan 1969/2008
Number of stones sent: 1
Addressees
Sent to *Dadakan's 88th Birthday Exhibition: Releasing Demon*
Asked to participate in this commemorative exhibition by Uehara Seiichirō, I send a *Stone* as an homage to Itoi Kanji, aka Dadakan.

2008.9.23–12.14
On Location, Sainsbury Centre for Visual Arts, Norwich, U.K.
Two *Stones* in the collection of Tate Archive are exhibited (Fig. 23). My wife and I visit Norwich and travel in England and France.

On Location: Siting Robert Smithson and His Contemporaries (p. 126)

2008.10.29
http://www.theguardian.com/artanddesign/2008/oct/29/1000-artworks-to-see-before-you-die-art

My *Stone* in the collection of Getty Research Institute

Fig. 23   *The Shinano River Plan 2000 and The Shinano River Plan 2001*, 2000+2001
オン・ロケーション展でテート・アーカイブ所蔵の《石》を展示
= *Stone* in the collection of Tate Archive, on view at *On Location*

2008–09
『石を送るメール・アート40周年記念』の冊子を発行
しようと構想を立てるが実現に至らず。

2009.3.31
**作品集『GUN 雪のイメージを変えるイベント1970
年2月11/15日』**
市橋哲夫、前山忠と3人で出資して発行。富井玲
子「GUNを世界に着地させる試み GUN Event to
Change the Image of Snow」を再録。

2009.4.1
The Shinano River Plan 2009
送付数：1
送付先
　新潟現代美術家集団GUNの軌跡展気付、椹木野衣宛
　（Fig. 24）

2009.4.6–12
新潟現代美術家集団GUNの軌跡展（トキ・アートスペー
ス、東京）

旧作と新作の《石》2点を展示する。

2009.5.28
「先進的アートを後世に GUNのイベント作品集に
して刊行」『上越タイムス』

2009.6.26
The Shinano River Plan 1969/2009
送付数：1
送付先
　彦坂尚嘉

以前のものはなくしたのでもう一度送ってほしいとの
要請があり、2個目を送る。

2009.7.21
《石を送るメール・アート》40周年記念 *The Shinano
River Plan 1969/2009*
送付数：5
送付先
　中原佑介（兵庫県立美術館館長）

---

is named one of "1000 artworks to see before you die:
Where to find them" by *The Guardian* (alphabetized
under "M" in the section "From the Maya to Diego
Rivera").

2008 onward
I collaborate with volunteers in the Nakasato and Matsudai areas to organize *Mountain Sleighs Project* as an
event for *Snow Art* at Echigo-Tsumari Art Field.

2008–09
I plan to publish a booklet, 40th Anniversary of *Mail
Art by Sending Stones*, but it is unrealized.

2009.3.31
*GUN: Event to Change the Image of Snow 1970 Feb.
11/15*, self-published [J/E]

Together with Ichihashi Tetsuo and Maeyama Tadashi,
I publish the portfolio of photographs with Reiko
Tomii's "An Attempt to Land GUN in World Art His-
tory: GUN's Event to Change the Image of Snow."

2009.4.1
The Shinano River Plan 2009

Number of stones sent: 1
Addressees
　Sawaragi Noi in care of *Trajectory of GUN: Niigata
　Contemporary Artists Collective* (Fig. 24)

2009.4.6–12
*Trajectory of GUN: Niigata Contemporary Artists Collec-
tive*, Toki Art Space, Tokyo
　I present 1 new and 1 old *Stone*.

2009.5.28
"Advanced Art for Posterity: Publication of GUN's
Event Portfolio," *Jōetsu Times* [J]

2009.6.26
The Shinano River Plan 1969/2009
Number of stones sent: 1
Addressees
　Hikosaka Naoyoshi

I send a second *Stone* upon his request, because he had
lost the one previously sent to him.

2009.7.21
40th Anniversary of Mail Art by Sending Stones: The

北川フラム（新潟市美術館館長）
グレン・ロワリー
　（ニューヨーク近代美術館館長）(Fig. 25)
リチャード・アームストロング
　（グッケンハイム美術館館長）
本人

後日、富井玲子がグッケンハイム美術館に届いているのを資料調査の際に確認する。

2009.7
大地の芸術祭に《Sky Catcher '09》を出品（松之山大厳寺高原）。

2009.9.11
The Shinano River Plan 1969/2009
送付数：1
送付先
　BankART 池田修

2009.10.14
府中美術館の、多摩川で／多摩川から、アートする展で、初めて高松次郎の《石と数字》の実物を見る。

2009.11.12
富井玲子「雪のイメージを変えるイベントと精神生理学研究所」『アート・オン・ペーパー』（82–83 頁）[E]

2009.8 以降
ブルー・スカイ・プロジェクト 2009 展にニューヨークから参加した砂入博史の《ツリー・プロジェクト》の柿の種が芽を出したので自宅に植樹し守り育てている。

2010
The Shinano River Plan 1969/2010
送付数：1
送付先
　ギャラリー花地蔵（上越市）での個展に出品

画廊主・福島武久あてに送る。

Shinano River Plan 1969/2009
Number of stones sent: 5
Addressees
　Nakahara Yūsuke, director,
　　Hyōgo Prefectural Museum of Art
　Kitagawa Fram, director, Niigata City Art Museum
　Glenn Lowry, director,
　　The Museum of Modern Art (Fig. 25)
　Richard Armstrong, director,
　　Guggenheim Museum
　Myself

Reiko Tomii subsequently confirms that the *Stone* sent to Guggenheim was duly received.

2009.7
I show *Sky Catcher '09* at Matsunoyama Daigonji Highland for the Echigo-Tsumari Triennial.

2009.8 onward
For his participation in *Blue Sky Project 2009*, Sunairi Hiroshi in New York contributes *Tree Project*, for which I planted a persimmon seed on his behalf. Since it has successfully sprouted, I decide to grow it.

2009.9.11
The Shinano River Plan 1969/2009
Number of stones sent: 1
Addressees
　Ikeda Osamu at BankART

2009.10.14
I see Takamatsu Jirō's *Stone and Numeral* in person for the first time in *At/From Tamagawa 1964–2009* at Fuchū Art Museum, Tokyo.

2009.11.12
Reiko Tomii, "Event to Change the Image of Snow and Psychophysiology Research Institute," *Art on Paper* (pp. 82–83)

2009 onward
Tree Project: In 2009, I join Sunairi Hiroshi's project and plant a persimmon seed to grow a tree. Separately, following the planting of a persimmon tree at Sanjō City's Tsukioka Elementary School in 2000, as part of Miyajima Tatsuo's *Kaki Tree Project*, I grow a persimmon tree from 2020, using a seed from the school's tree.

Fig. 24 *The Shinano River Plan 2009*, 2009
トキ・アートスペースの新潟現代美術家集団GUNの軌跡展気付で椹木野衣に送った《石》
= *Stone* sent to Sawaragi Noi in care of Toki Art Space's exhibition *Trajectory of GUN: Niigata Contemporary Artists Collective*

Fig. 25 《石を送るメール・アート》40周年記念 *The Shinano River Plan 1969/2009*
= *40th Anniversary of Mail Art by Sending Stones: The Shinano River Plan 1969/2009*, 2009
MoMAに送った《石》の到着と所在は不明 = *Stone* sent to MoMA, whereabouts unknown

2010.5.31
銀座のギャラリー Q の鈴木慶則個展会場で『美術手帖』元編集長の宮澤壮佳に初めて会い、《The Shinano River Plan:11-2》と《The Shinano River Plan: 12》の2点を大切に保管していることを伺う。

2011.4–2013.3
この2年間《E-Stamps Series》で月刊雑誌『先駆』の表紙を24回担当。
（この頃に《E-mail Stamps Series》を《E-Stamps Series》に短縮。作品には E-mail から E-Stamp とタイプするようになる。）

2011.6.29–30
日本美術オーラル・ヒストリー・アーカイヴによる「前山忠・堀川紀夫（新潟現代美術家集団 GUN）オーラル・ヒストリー」のインタビューを上越市の前山忠宅にて行う。インタヴュアーは、高晟埈と宮田有香。2016年と2019年に http://www.oralarthistory.org で公開。

2011.7.21
The Shinano River Plan 1969/2011

送付数：1
送付先
　徳永健一（新潟県立美術館館長）

2012年の同館の GUN 展開催計画とリンクして送る。

2011.12
富井玲子「東京ビエンナーレ1970年にむかって：国際時代における『国際的同時性』の形」
『レビュー・オブ・ジャパニーズ・カルチャー・アンド・ソサエティ』（城西大学英文紀要）[E]

2011.12.8
The Shinano River Plan 1969/2011
送付数：1
送付先
　石井孝之（Taka-Ishii Gallery）

《雪のイメージを変えるイベント》ポートフォリオを購入していただいた縁で送る。

2010
The Shinano River Plan 1969/2010
Number of stones sent: 1
Addressees
　Sent to my solo exhibition at Gallery Hanajizō, Jōetsu

I send a *Stone* in care of Fukushima Takehisa, gallery owner.

2010.5.31
At Suzuki Yoshinori's solo exhibition at Gallery Q in Ginza, Tokyo, I meet for the first time with Miyazawa Takeyoshi, a former chief editor of *Bijutsu techō*. I learn that he has preserved my *The Shinano River Plan: 11-2* and *The Shinano River Plan: 12*.

2011.4–2013.3
I create 24 cover images with *E-Stamps Series* for the monthly magazine *Senku* (Pioneer) for 2 years. Around this time, I change the series title from *E-mail Stamps Series* to *E-Stamps Series*. Accordingly, I include the word "E-Stamp" in the retitled series, instead of "E-mail."

2011.6. 29–30
Maeyama Tadashi and I are interviewed by Koh Seong-Jun and Miyata Yūka at Maeyama's home for Oral History Archive of Japanese Art. Transcripts are uploaded in 2016 and 2019 at http://www.oralarthistory.org.

2011.7.21
The Shinano River Plan 1969/2011
Number of stones sent: 1
Addressees
　Tokunaga Ken'ichi, director,
　　Niigata Prefectural Museum of Modern Art

I send a *Stone* in preparation for GUN's retrospective at the museum in 2012.

2011.12
Reiko Tomii, "Toward Tokyo Biennale 1970: Shapes of the International in the Age of 'International Contemporaneity,'" *Review of Japanese Culture and Society*

2011.12.8
The Shinano River Plan 1969/2011
Number of stones sent: 1

2011.12.10

府中市美術館の石子順造的世界展のオープニングで宮澤壯佳が保管している2つの《石》を見せていただく。箱に入れられて極めて良好に保管された姿に感謝感激する。来場していた石井孝之、富井玲子もこれを目撃。

2012.1.1

The Shinano River Plan 1969/2012

送付数：1
送付先
　大久保淳二

1986年に大久保淳二に送った石の荷札がペットのウサギに食べられたことから、《石》を預かってきて、このシリーズでもユニークな初の「送り直し」となった（Fig. 26）。大久保は癌で闘病中。その病中見舞をかねて回復を願う意味もあった。しかしその後急激に病状が悪化し逝去。

2012.11.3–2013.1.14

GUN──新潟に前衛があった頃展（新潟県立近代美術館）

旧作の「石」4点（送付先：徳永健一、本人、宮澤壯佳の2点）および手元にある全関係資料が展示される。

| 　カタログ

2012.12.8

富井玲子『現代美術の地平に石を探る 堀川紀夫の《石のメール・アート》』BAKU出版局刊
BAKUは自家出版用名称。〔論考1として本書に再録〕

2013.2

塩田純一「ベールを脱いだ地方の前衛：『GUN 新潟に前衛があった頃』展」『美術手帖』（170頁）

2013.8.6

The Shinano River Plan 1969/2013

送付数：1
送付先
　小田原ビエンナーレ2013に出品

ビエンナーレ主宰の飯室哲也気付けで送る。

Addressees
　Ishii Takayuki, Taka Ishii Gallery

I send a *Stone* in thanks for his purchase of the portfolio of *Event to Change the Image of Snow*.

2011.12.10

I meet with Miyazawa Takeyoshi at the opening of *The World of Ishiko Junzō* at Fuchū Art Museum. He brings 2 *Stones* in his collection to show me. I am very thankful that he has preserved them in a box in an extremely good condition. Ishii Takayuki and Reiko Tomii are also at the opening and see them.

2012.1.1

The Shinano River Plan 1969/2012
Number of stones sent: 1
Addressees
　Ōkubo Junji

The mail tag attached to the *Stone* sent to Ōkubo in 1985 was eaten by his pet rabbit, so I borrow his *Stone* and undertake the first "resending," unique in *Mail Art by Sending Stones* (Fig. 26). It is also intended as a "get well" gift to Ōkubo who is then fighting cancer. Un-

fortunately, his condition quickly deteriorates and he passes away on February 7.

2012.11.3–2013.1.14

GUN: Niigata Contemporary Artists Group and Its Era, Niigata Prefectural Museum of Modern Art
The exhibition includes 4 old *Stones* sent to Tokunaga Ken'ichi, myself, and Miyazawa Takeyoshi (2 *Stones*), along with all related documents.

| Catalogue

2012.12.8

Reiko Tomii, *Exploring Stones on the Horizon of Contemporary Art: Horikawa Michio's Mail Art by Sending Stones*, pub. Baku Publishing [J]

Baku Publishing is my self-publishing imprint. [Translated into English and included in this volume as Text 1.]

2013.2

Shioda Jun'ichi, "Regional Avant-Garde Unveiled: GUN: Niigata Contemporary Artist Group and Its Era," *Bijutsu techō* (p. 170) [J]

2013.11.5–25
小田原ビエンナーレ 2013 に《石》と《E-Stamps Series》を 200 点ほど出品。

2013.12.8
The Shinano River Plan 1969/2013
送付数：1
送付先
　人間と物質展再展示計画シンポジウムに出品

同シンポジウム企画者の成相肇気付で送る（Fig. 27）。

2013.12.28
森美術館での人間と物質展再展示計画シンポジウムに出席し、《石》について再評価を受けて再開している旨を話した。

2013
　佐藤拓真「ここ／そこ／どこか──もの派以降の芸術における場」修士論文（横浜国立大学都市イノベーション学府）

東京ビエンナーレに出品した《石》が論述されている（47–48 頁）。

2014.6.17
富井玲子から、松澤宥宅での資料調査の折りに《石を送るメール・アート》第 1 号を発見したとメールあり。ニルヴァーナ展で配った荷札付き 5 円玉とともに大切に保管されていたとのこと。

2014
静岡県立美術館のグループ「幻触」と石子順造展に《The Shinano River Plan: 12》の石子関係資料を展示。
　カタログに図版掲載（184–185 頁）

2014.7.21
The Shinano River Plan 1969/2014
送付数：1
送付先
　塩田純一

新潟市美術館館長就任を記念して送る（Fig. 28）。塩田

2013.8.6
The Shinano River Plan 1969/2013
Number of stones sent: 1
Addressees
　Sent to *Odawara Biennale 2013*

I send a *Stone* in care of Iida Tetsuya, the biennale's organizer.

2013.11.5–25
I present *Mail Art by Sending Stones* and some 200 works of *E-Stamps Series* at Odawara Biennale 2013.

2013.12.8
The Shinano River Plan 1969/2013
Number of stones sent: 1
Addressees
　Sent to "Symposium in Preparation of Restaging of *Between Man and Matter*"

I send a *Stone* in care of Nariai Hajime, the symposium organizer (Fig. 27).

2013.12.28
I give a talk about the resumption of *Stones* thanks to

the recent recognition at "Symposium in Preparation of Restaging of *Between Man and Matter*" held at Mori Art Museum, Tokyo.

2013
　Satō Takuma, "Here, There, Where: Sites of Art of Mono-ha and After," master's thesis, Institute of Urban Innovation, Yokohama [J]

My *Stones* in *Tokyo Biennale 1970* is discussed (pp. 47–48).

2014.6.17
Reiko Tomii e-mails me from her research at the late Matsuzawa Yutaka's residence, reporting that she found 1 of the first *Stones* from the July 1969 mailing. It is preserved in a good condition, along with the five-yen coin I distributed in the Matsuzawa-organized *Nirvana* exhibition.

2014
The document related to Ishiko Junzō from *The Shinano River Plan: 12* is exhibited in *Group "Genshoku"and Ishiko Junzō* at Shizuoka Prefectural Museum of Art.

Fig. 26　*The Shinano River Plan 1969/2012*, 2012
　　　　大久保淳二宛の《石》は「送り直し」第1号 = *Stone* sent to Ōkubo Junji as the unique "resending"

Fig. 27　*The Shinano River Plan 1969/2013*, 2013
　　　　「人間と物質展再現計画シンポジウム」に送った《石》
　　　　= *Stone* sent to "Symposium in Preparation of Restaging of *Between Man and Matter*"

とは、宮島達男の《柿の木プロジェクト》に関係する縁があった。

2014.8.15
| アライ＝ヒロユキ『天皇アート論——その美"天"に通ず』社会評論社刊
天皇をテーマとした Stamp 作品が言及される（122–123 頁）。

2015.1
| 『E-Stamp Series』自家出版
月刊「先駆」表紙作品を中心にした作品集（11 部限定）。

2015.8.1—8.30
帯広コンテンポラリーアート 2015 マイナスアート展に、帯広市在住の池田緑との縁で参加。《Snow Performance》出品。

| 『マイナスアート展』図録　帯広コンテンポラリーアート実行委員会（184–185 頁）

2015 以降
テンセグリティに出会いその基本を自学でマスター。《Tensegrity Series》として展開している。

2016
| 富井玲子『荒野のラジカリズム：国際的同時性と日本の 1960 年代美術』マサチューセッツ工科大学出版会刊 [E]

富井玲子と 6 月 4 日に東京で面会し、献本 1 冊を受ける。その同じ日に同著を読んだアメリカの宇宙開発関係研究者ティーゼル・エリザベス・ムイア＝ハーモニーからメールがある。その後ムイア＝ハーモニーが北陸新幹線にて堀川宅へ《石》についてインタビューにくる。

2016.5.28
| エドワード・M・ゴメス「日本、荒野の：富井玲子の拡張した近代美術史」『Hyperallegic.com』[E]

2016.7.4
| 「石のメール・アート再評価」『上越よみうり』
富井の著書やムイア＝ハーモニーによる取材などの紹介。

| Catalogue: illustrated (pp. 184–85) [J]

2014.7.21
The Shinano River Plan 1969/2014
Number of stones sent: 1
Addressees
　　Shioda Jun'ichi

I send a *Stone* to congratulate Shioda's appointment as director of Niigata City Art Museum (Fig. 28). I knew him via Miyajima Tatsuo's *Kaki Tree Project*. I planted two persimmon trees descended from an A-bombed tree at Sanjō City Elementary School, where I was principal, to commemorate that year's graduating class in February 2000.

2014.8.15
| Arai Hiroyuki, *Critique of Art about Tenno Emperor System: Beauty of Universalism and Nature*, pub. Shakai Hyōronsha (pp. 122–23) [J]

My emperor-themed Stamps are discussed (pp. 122–23).

2015.1
| *E-Stamp Series*, self-published [J]

A compilation mainly of the cover images for *Senku* (edition of 11).

2015.8.1–8.30
I participate in *Minus Art: Obihiro Contemporary Art 2015* thanks to my association with Ikeda Midori, a resident of Obihiro. I present *Snow Performance*.

| *Minus-Art*, pub. Obihiro Contemporary Art Exhibition Committee [J]

2015 onward
Upon discovery of "tensegrity," I taught myself its principles and since create *Tensegrity Series*.

2016
| Reiko Tomii, *Radicalism in the Wilderness: International Contemporaneity and 1960s Art in Japan*, pub. MIT Press

On June 4, I meet with Tomii in Tokyo and receive a copy. On the very same day, I receive an e-mail from Teasel Elizabeth Muir-Harmony, an American researcher of space exploration. She subsequently visits me at home via the Hokuriku bullet train and inter-

2016.7.21
《石を送るメール・アート》47 周年 *The Shinano River Plan 1969/2016*
送付数：1
送付先
　本人

2016.11
本阿弥清『〈もの派〉の起源』水声社刊 （91–92 頁）

2017
伊村靖子「精神生理学研究所――メディア論としての作家表現」『NACT Review 国立新美術館研究紀要』4 号（図版 4）

2018
富井玲子「荒野からの呼び声：GUN の雪のイメージを変えるイベント」『荒野』シルン・クンストハレ（フランクフルト）刊 （92–101 頁）[E]

2018.7.21
《石を送るメール・アート》48 周年 *The Shinano River Plan 1969/2018*
送付数：1
送付先
　辛美沙（Misa Shin Gallery）

2018.9.28–11.10
Misa Shin Gallery で個展「Not a Stone's Throw」を開催（Fig. 29）。BT などのウエブサイトで案内される。この個展で初めて《石》が売れた。米国のコレクターだった。富井玲子が付けてくれたタイトルは「a stone's throw ＝石を投げたら届くほどの至近距離」の反語的借用。《石を送るメール・アート》の物語に新しい章節が付け足されたようだった。

2018.10.24
アライ・ヒロユキ「美術『Not a Stone's Throw』石が問う想像の秘めた力」『しんぶん赤旗』

---

views me about *Mail Art by Sending Stones*.

2016.5.28
Edward M. Gómez, "Japan, in from the Wilderness: Reiko Tomii's Expanded Modern-Art History," *Hyperallegic.com*

2016.7.4
"Reassessment of Mail Art by Sending Stones," *Jōetsu Yomiuri* [J]

The article reports on Tomii's book and Muir-Harmony's visit.

2016.7.21
47th Anniversary of Mail Art by Sending Stones: The Shinano River Plan 1969/2016
Number of stones sent: 1
Addressees
　Myself

2016.11
Honnami Kiyoshi, *The Origin of Mono-ha*, published by Suiseisha (pp. 91–92) [J]

2017
Iniwa Yasuko, "Psychophysiology Research Institute (Seishin Seirigaku Kenkyūjo): Artistic Expression as Media Theory," *NACT Review*, no. 4 (fig. 4) [J]

2018
Reiko Tomii, "A Call from the Wilderness: GUN's *Event to Change the Image of Snow*," in *Wilderness*, pub. Schirn Kunsthalle Frankfurt (pp. 92–101)

2018.7.21
48th Anniversary of Mail Art by Sending Stones: The Shinano River Plan 1969/2018
Number of stones sent: 1
Addressees
　Shin Misa (Misa Shin Gallery)

2018.9.28–11.10
Not a Stone's Throw, Misa Shin Gallery, Tokyo (Fig. 29)
My solo exhibition is announced online including the website of *Bijutsu techo*. From this solo exhibition, *a Stone* is for the first time sold. It is acquired by a U.S. collector. The title, conceived by Reiko Tomii, alludes to "distance" in mail art as opposed to the proximity of "a stone's throw." I feel that a new chapter is added to

Fig. 28   *The Shinano River Plan 1969/2014*, 2014
            45周年記念の《石》= *Stone* marking the 45th anniversary

Fig. 29   Misa Shin Gallery 開催の《石》の個展の展示風景
            = *Stone* featured in my solo exhibition at Misa Shin Gallery

2019.1.1
The Shinano River Plan 1969/2019
送付数：1
送付先
　ジャパン・ソサエティ代表

荒野のラジカリズム展への出品作品として送る。

2019.3
　佐藤秀治「時の忘れもの：時の 131：アポロ 11 号」
　『My Skip』

2019.3.8–6.9
荒野のラジカリズム：グローバル 1960 年代の日本の
美術家たち展（ジャパン・ソサエティ、ニューヨーク）に出品。
企画は富井玲子と神谷幸江（ジャパン・ソサエティ・ギャラ
リー・ディレクター）。《石を送るメール・アート》は、旧
作の石 4 個（送付先：松沢宥、宮澤壮佳 2 個、前山忠）と新
しい石 2 個（グッゲンハイム美術館、ジャパン・ソサエティ）
のほか、データカードや映像を展示（Figs. 30.1–2）。《ゼ
ロ円切手》、《絵葉書》シリーズや GUN《雪のイメー

ジを変えるイベント》など 30 点以上を出品。

　ニューヨークへ夫婦で訪れ、作品の生成から半世紀
を経て大いなる節目を刻むことができた。ワールド・
トレード・センターのメモリアルを巡礼、フィラデル
フィア美術館やディア・ビーコンなどで美術館研修を
深める。

荒野のラジカリズム展関連出版物 ────────

│　展覧会パンフレット [E]

2019.3
　リー・アン・ミラー「裏話：堀川紀夫の抗議の石」『アー
　ト・イン・アメリカ』（35 頁）[E]

2019.3.15
　ジョナサン・キーツ「このスリリングなジャパン・
　ソサエティの展覧会で、日本の地方作家がいかに
　ニール・アームストロングの上を行ったか」『Forbes.
　com』[E]
　〔展評 1 として和訳を本書再録〕

---

the story of *Mail Art by Sending Stones*.

2018.10.24
　Arai Hiroyuki, "Art: Not a Stone's Throw: Stones
　Challenge Hidden Creative Power," *Shinbun Aka-
　hata* [J]

2019.1.1
The Shinano River Plan 1969/2019
Number of stones sent: 1
Addressees
　Japan Society president

I send a Stone in conjunction with *Radicalism in the
Wilderness* exhibition.

2019.3
　Satō Hideharu, "Things Forgotten by Time, 131:
　Apollo 11," *My Skip* [J]

2019.3.8–6.9
My works are included in *Radicalism in the Wilderness:
Japanese Artists in the Global 1960s* at Japan Society
in New York. It is curated by Reiko Tomii and Yukie
Kamiya (director, Japan Society Gallery). Selected

from *Mail Art by Sending Stones* are 4 old *Stones*, sent
to Matsuzawa Yutaka, Miyazawa Takeyoshi (2 *Stones*),
and Maeyama Tadashi, as well as 2 new *Stones*, sent to
Guggenheim Museum and Japan Society; a selection
of data cards and a slide show are also shown (Figs.
30.1–2). The total of more than 30 works is presented in
the GUN section, including *Event to Change the Image
of Snow*, along with my *Zero-Yen Stamps* and *Postcards*,
among others.

　My wife and I visit New York to mark the 50 years
of my *Stones* since the birth of this series. We also visit
the 9/11 Memorial & Museum, the Philadelphia Museum of Art, and Dia: Beacon.

Related Publications to
Radicalism in the Wilderness ───────────

│　Exhibition brochure

2019.3
│　Leigh Anne Miller, "Backstory: Protest Rock by
│　Horikawa Michio," *Art in America* (p. 35)

2019.3.15
│　Jonathon Keats, "See How a Provincial Japanese

Fig. 30.1–2　ジャパン・ソサエティで開催された荒野のラジカリズム展の展示風景。
　　　　　　新旧の《石》にくわえて、壁にはデータカードや写真、スライドショーが展示された
　　　　　　= *Stones*, old and new, along with data cards, photographs, and a slide show,
　　　　　　　presented at *Radicalism in the Wilderness* (Japan Society)

2019.4.12
ジェーソン・ファラーゴ「展評：東京の喧騒からはるか遠く」『ニューヨーク・タイムズ』[E]

2019.4.20
富井玲子「GUN における行為と情報──荒野のラジカリズム展補遺」『美術運動史』172 号
〔論考 2 として改訂して本書再録〕

2019.5.22
「新潟発の作品 米で話題『本場で知られてうれしい』」『新潟日報』

2019.6.18
藤森愛実「歴史を映した意思と感性 ニューヨーク『荒野のラジカリズム』展」『朝日新聞』夕刊

――――――――――

2019.7.21
《石を送るメール・アート》50 周年メモリアル
The Shinano River Plan 1969/2019

送付数：6
送付先
　ハワード・ラチョフスキー
　アルフレッド・ジャー
　島敦彦
　植松奎二
　堀川紀幸（東京在住、息子）
　本人

アメリカへ 2 個、国内へ 3 個の《石》を送る（Figs. 31, 33）。一つの表現のコンセプトが 50 年持ちこたえたことを自賛した。
　ラチョフスキーは《The Shinano River Plan: 12》のコレクターでテキサス州ダラス在住。ジャーとは、荒野のラジカリズム展のオープニングのためにニューヨークを訪れて、20 年ぶりに会う。アトリエ訪問でお寿司のご馳走にもなった。2000 年の第 1 回大地の芸術祭の《小さな美術館》に GUN の《雪のイメージを変えるイベント》が選ばれたことが GUN の活動をまとめることへの引き金になったと振り返っている。島とは富山県立近代美術館の日本海美術展で知己を得る。

Artist Bested Neil Armstrong At This Thrilling Japan Society Exhibit," *Forbes.com*
[Reprinted in this volume as Review 1]

2019.4.12
Jason Farago, "Art Review: Far from the Tumult of Tokyo," *New York Times*

2019.4.20
Reiko Tomii, "GUN's Act and Information: Reflection at *Radicalism in the Wilderness*," *Bijutsu undōshi*, no. 172 [J]
[Revised, translated into English, and included in this volume as Text 2]

2019.5.22
"Art from Niigata: Shown in the U.S., 'Glad to Show at the Art World Center,'" *Niigata nippō* [J]

2019.6.18
Manami Fujimori, "Will and Sensibility Reflecting History: *Radicalism in the Wilderness* in New York," *Asahi shinbun*, evening edition [J]

――――――――――

2019.7.21
50th Anniversary of Mail Art by Sending Stones: The Shinano River Plan 1969/2019
Number of stones sent: 6
Addressees
　Howard Rachofsky
　Alfredo Jaar
　Shima Atsuhiko
　Uematsu Keiji
　Horikawa Michiyuki (son, in Tokyo)
　Myself

I send 2 *Stones* to the U.S. and 3 *Stones* within Japan to celebrate the fact that a single idea has maintained its relevance for 50 years (Figs. 31, 33).
　Rachofsky in Dallas is a collector of *The Shinano River Plan: 12*. I meet Jaar for the first time after 20 years. I visit him at his studio, and he treats me to a sushi dinner. I am grateful for his inclusion of GUN's *Event to Change the Image of Snow* in *Bunka no Hako*, his contribution to the first Echigo-Tsumari Triennial in 2000, which inspired me to organize GUN's materials for publication. I came to know Shima at the time of *Sea of Japan Exhibition* at Toyama Prefectural Museum of Art and Design. He subsequently came to see *32*

その後、旧長岡現代美術館で開催された新潟現代美術32人展に来ていただいた。植松は、1972年8月の部分展で一緒する。2009年の大地の芸術祭で、松之山大厳寺キャンプ場の野外展示で植松作品の隣の位置に拙作《Sky Catcher '09》が設置された。その後、荒野のラジカリズム展のオープニングでお会いする。

2019.8.1

「米国ニューヨークで"日本の現代美術家"展 前山忠さん、堀川紀夫さん 報告会開く」『上越タイムス』

2020.6.26

アレックス・キトニック「石の作品：アース・アートが郵便局に行った時」『4Colunms.com』[E]
〔展評2として和訳を本書再録〕

2019 秋

ティーゼル・エリザベス・ムイア＝ハーモニー「宇宙時代におけるアメリカ合衆国の科学外交の限度」
『パシフィック・ヒストリカル・レビュー』（615–16頁）[E]

2020.7.21

石を送るメール・アート51周年 The Shinano River Plan 1969/2020
送付数：1
送付先
　長女家族（関裕太郎、美紀、晴生、俊輔）

2020

《石》の50年の歩みをまとめる作業を本格的に開始。

2020 以降

2019年の11月に、三条市月岡小学校で2000年に植樹した宮島達男の柿の木プロジェクトの実をいただいてきた。その種が芽を出したので育て始める。

2021.2 以降

フォトショップで描くデジタル絵画《CG-Automatism Series》を展開。SNSで発表。

2021.3.9

|「上越の美術家・堀川紀夫さん『石を送るメール・アー

Contemporary Artists in Niigata held at the former site of Museum of Contemporary Art, Nagaoka. Uematsu and I both participated in the exhibition *Parts in August 1972. My Sky Catcher '09* was installed next to his work at Matsunoyama Daigonji Campsite for the 2009 Echigo-Tsumari Triennial, and I reconnect with him at the opening of *Radicalism in the Wilderness*.

2019.8.1

"Maeyama Tadashi and Horikawa Michio report on their participation in a Japanese contemporary art exhibition in New York," *Jōetsu Times* [J]

2019 fall

Teasel Elizabeth Muir-Harmony, "The Limits of U.S. Science Diplomacy in the Space Age," *Pacific Historical Review* (pp. 615–16)

2020.6.26

Alex Kitnick, "Stone Work: When Earth Art Hit the Mails," *4Colunms.com*
[Reprinted in this volume as Review 2]

2020.7.21

51st Anniversary of Mail Art by Sending Stones: The

Shinano River Plan 1969/2020
Number of stones sent: 1
Addressees
　My eldest daughter's family (Seki Yūtarō, Miki, Haruo, and Shunsuke)

2020

I begin an earnest effort to chronicle the past 50 years of *Stones*.

2020 onward

The persimmon trees to commemorate the class of 2003 at Tsukioka Elementary School in Sanjō have grown to yield seeds. Among the seeds I am given, one successfully sprouts and I decide to grow it.

2021.3.9

"Horikawa Michio, an Artist in Jōetsu: *Mail Art by Sending Stones* Rediscovered in the U.S., the Center of Contemporary Art, through Exhibition and Online News," *Niigata nippō*, Jōetsu edition [J]

2021.2 onward

I create *CG-Automatism Series*, for which I use Photoshop to paint digitally and present new works on social

Fig. 31　《石を送るメール・アート》50周年メモリアル *The Shinano River Plan 1969/2019*
= *50th Anniversary of Mail Art by Sending Stones: The Shinano River Plan 1969/2019*, 2019
ハワード・ラチョフスキー宛の《石》= *Stone* sent to Howard Rachofsky

Fig. 32　ドレスデンで《石を送るメール・アート》をビルボード展示
= *Mail Art by Sending Stones*, billboard installation at
Robotron Kantine in Dresden (curated by Miyo Yoshida)

2021.3.31

| 堀川紀夫「美術教師と作家の両道を紡いで」

ノルウエーのアートコレクティブ Carrie へ自己ドキュメンタリーを寄稿.

2021.7.21

《石》52 周年を迎える。

《石を送るメール・アート》52 周年 *The Shinano River Plan 1969/2021*

送付数：2
送付先
　菅章（大分市立美術館館長）
　次女家族（三瓶正彦、絵美、結菜、真菜穂）

管章は 1993 年の教育雑誌『美育文化』8 月号の特集「オブジェの衝撃」への寄稿者同士だった。2007 年のドクメンタ、ミュースター彫刻プロジェクト・ツアーでも一緒した。2019 年の磯崎新展で大分市美術館へ伺い館内を案内していただいた。

2021.11–2022.3

ポーランドの首都ワルシャワのザチェタ国立美術館の、集団と個人の間：1950–60 年代の日本の前衛展に《石》を出品。

2021–22

ドレスデン・クンストハウスの 30 周年記念企画で《石》が野外展示プロジェクトに選ばれる。タイトルは《Den Steinen zuhören／石に耳を澄ます／Listening to the Stones》（Fig. 32）。

2022.7.21

《石》53 周年を迎える。

『石を送るメール・アート：読本』を現代企画室より発行。

---

media.

2021.3.31

| Horikawa Michio, "Following Two Paths as an Art Teacher and an Artist" [J]

I contribute an autobiographical essay to Carrie, a Norwegian collective.

2021.7.21

Stones marks its 52nd anniversary.

52nd Anniversary of Mail Art by Sending Stones: The Shinano River Plan 1969/2021

Number of stones sent: 2
Addressees
　Suga Akira, director, Ōita Art Museum
　My second eldest daughter's family (Sanpe Masahiko, Emi, Yuina, and Manaho)

Both Suga Akira and I contributed to the special feature "The Shock of *Objets*" in the August 1993 issue of *Biiku bunka* (Art education and culture). In 2007, we were both on a tour group to visit Documenta and Munster Sculpture Project. In 2019, when I visited his museum to see Isozaki Arata's retrospective, he gave me a walkthrough.

2021.11–2022.3

Mail Art by Sending Stones is included in *Between Collectivism and Individualism: Japanese Avant-Garde of the 50s and 60s* at Zachęta National Gallery in Warsaw (Fig. 32).

2021–2022

My *Stones* are selected for an outdoor project as part of *Still Crazy: 30 Years Kunsthaus Dresden* in Dresden. The title is *Listening to the Stones*.

2022.7.21

Stones marks its 53rd anniversary.

I publish *Mail Art by Sending Stones: A Reader* from the Gendaikikakushitsu publishers.

(Translated from the Japanese original by the author)

Fig. 33　《石を送るメール・アート》50周年メモリアル *The Shinano River Plan 1969/2019*
= *50th Anniversary of Mail Art by Sending Stones: The Shinano River Plan 1969/2019*, 2019
本人宛の《石》= *Stone* sent to the artist himself

Related Works

関連アルバム

《E-Mail Stamp Series（広島の少女）》2008年
= *E-Mail Stamp Series (A Girl in Hiroshima)*, 2008

GUN《雪のイメージを変えるイベント》1970年
= GUN, *Event to Change the Image of Snow*, 1970

1970年2月11日と15日、新潟現代美術家集団GUNのメンバーたちは、写真撮影をした羽永光利らの協力・支援のもとに十日町を流れる信濃川の川原に繰り出し、ゴージャスなカラーフィールドの抽象絵画を描き出した。雪ですっぽりと覆われた川原は作家たちにとっては壮大なカンバスとなったが、雪国に暮らす住民にとっては、雪遊びを楽しむどころか、雪下ろしなど過酷な生活を象徴していた。困難な日常の時間に一瞬なりとも「わあ、すごい」という嬉しい驚きを演出したいというのが彼らの目的だった。衝撃的な顔料の散布行為を撮りたいという写真家たちの意欲を感じて、堀川紀夫は褌姿で雪原を赤く染める単独の行為を行った。また、自分の背丈よりも高く積もった雪に身体を刻印する行為も行い、1980年代に展開する《Snow Performance》を予告することにもなった。

——富井玲子

On February 11 and 15, 1970, the members of GUN (Group Ultra Niigata) spread out onto a dry riverbed of the Shinano River in Tōkamachi and spray-painted a gorgeous color-field abstraction. The vast area of the riverbed formed an enticing blank canvas when thickly covered by snow. It had occupied their minds for some time. In the region known for the heaviest snow in the country, the snow-covered fields, still being blanketed by falling snow, was less a joyous playground than a reminder of the burdens such severe weather brought to everyday life. Their goal was to transform a hardship into a pleasant surprise. Additionally, the photographers' desire to capture a shocking act of spraying paint inspired Horikawa to stage a solo act by wearing a loincloth alone and staining the snow field red. He also made imprints of his body on a pile of snow higher than his head, which he would later develop as *Snow Performance* in the 1980s.

—— Reiko Tomii

GUN《雪のイメージを変えるイベント》（堀川紀夫の単独行為）1970年
= GUN, *Event to Change the Image of Snow* (Horikawa Michio's solo act), 1970

GUN《雪のイメージを変えるイベント》（堀川紀夫の単独行為）1970年
= GUN, *Event to Change the Image of Snow* (Horikawa Michio's solo act), 1970

《Snow Performance（2つの人型）》1983年
= *Snow Performance '83-F2*, 1983

《Snow Performance（人型と影）》1983年
= *Snow Performance '83-F*, 1983

雪面に残された人体の刻印は、その深さという点ではプリントでなく促成のレリーフといったほうがふさわしい。〔中略〕写真に残されているのは雪面のレリーフである。しかし、このレリーフそのものは一時的なものであって、それは雪の溶解とともに姿を消す。身を投げ出す行為があり、非永続的な形態がうまれ、写真を撮るという行為があり、写真が残る。堀川の行ったのはそういうことだが、パフォーマンス、その結果として視覚的な形態を残すという過程そのものは、芸術表現のオーソドックスともいえるものであって、特別なことではない。独特なのは、堀川紀夫のそれが雪面で行われたという点である。

──中原佑介
『Snow Performance』1993 年より抜粋

The imprint of the human form on the snow could be more suitably called "instant relief" than "print." ... Horikawa's "reliefs on the snow" are captured in photographs, but the reliefs themselves were temporary and disappeared with the snow. The act of throwing himself onto the snow produced impermanent forms, but the pictures taken upon the snow left permanent images. However, performances resulting in visual structure constitute a purely orthodox artistic expression. In this sense, nothing is unique. The uniqueness of Horikawa's art consists in performing on the snow.

── Nakahara Yūsuke
Excerpted from *Snow Performance* (1993)

《零円切手（佐藤栄作）》1971年
= *Zero-Yen Stamp (Satō Eisaku)*, 1971

堀川紀夫はGUNの名前で佐藤栄作総理大臣の顔をあしらっ
た零円切手第一号を発行。1971年3月20日付の機関紙『GUN』
第2号で「日々の郵送ゲリラ戦に活用」するよう檄を飛ばし
ている。ちなみにこの作品には「帝国主義無能者像」のコメ
ントが入っている。

——富井玲子

Under the banner of GUN, Horikawa published the first *Zero-Yen Stamp* with the face of Prime Minister Satō Eisaku. In its newsletter, dated March 20, 1971, the group urged the readers to use *Zero-Yen Stamp* in their "daily guerrilla acts" of the "Postal Mailing Front." Horikawa included a mocking comment, "the portrait of an incompetent imperialist," in his stamp.

—— Reiko Tomii

《E-Stamp Series（トルーマンの切手）》2020＋2021＋2022年
＝ *E-Stamp Series*, 2020+2021+2022

広島・長崎原爆投下後77年を過ぎたが、この3年間で原爆症で亡くなられる方を数えると1日20名以上で
続いている ＝ Seventy seven years have passed since the dropping of atomic bombs on Hiroshima and Nagasaki.
For the past three years, more than twenty people passed away every day due to ailments related to the A-bombs.

Review 1
Jonathon Keats

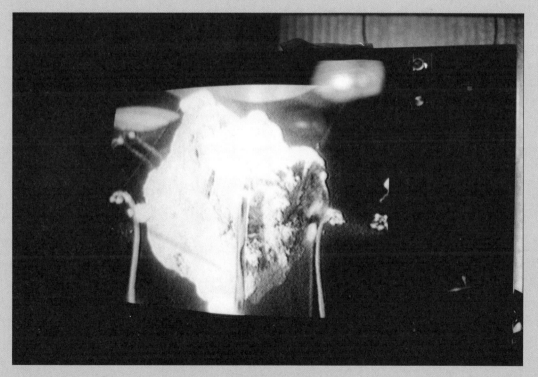

1970.12.31

NHKテレビの年末回顧番組で「月の石」を撮影。大阪万博では長蛇の列で見ることができなかった

= I photograph a "moon rock" shown in NHK's yearend program on memorable events that year. It was shown at *Expo '70* in Osaka, but I decided not to see it because of the long waiting line.

ニール・アームストロングの上を行った日本の地方作家

ジョナサン・キーツ

　ニール・アームストロングとバズ・オルドリンが月面に降り立ったとき、主要任務の一つとして月の石を集めた。その着陸の瞬間、堀川紀夫という日本の作家が新潟の信濃川に中学1年生の生徒たちを連れて行き、石集めを手伝うように指示した。彼らは集めた石を地元の郵便局へ持っていき、そこで堀川は石に針金を巻き付け、荷札を付け、自分の仲間の作家たちに送った。

　堀川の《石を送るメール・アート》は1960年代日本におけるコンセプチュアル・アートの独創的な作品だが、西洋ではまだほとんど知られていない。ニューヨークのジャパンソ・ソサエティで開かれた展覧会《荒野のラジカリズム》は重要な展観だ。こうした歴史の見落しを正し、堀川にくわえて前山忠、松澤宥など60年代コンセプチャリズムを考えるのに欠かせない作家たちに焦点をあてている。

　同展の出品作家のうち、もっとも突出した存在は松澤で、作品もなく観客もいない展覧会を企画した。より正確に言うなら、参加作家たちが作品を展示し観客がそれに出会うために松澤が考案した方法は、従来の物理的経験の埒外にあるのだ。松澤の出した雑誌広告にいわく、「あなたの出品物はあなたの手元に置いて、それから発する無形のもの（虚の作品）を会場まで届けてください」、「出品希望者は直ちに有形無形の連絡を始めてください」。

　展示会場が東京から遥かに遠い荒野だったことを思えば、松澤が参加者への物理的要求を最低限に抑えたことは疑いなく巧妙なアイディアだった。しかし「荒野におけるアンデパンダン'64展」は、野心的な地方作家にとって単なる戦略的回避策以上のものだった。ソル・ルウィットのような西洋のコンセプチュアル作家が、他者による作品制作の規則を提示して美術作品を非物質化するはるか以前に、松澤はアートに必要なのは一個の焦点を共有することだけだと喝破したのだ。アートの本質は、人々の間の関係性であり、モノは便宜的道具としての役割を果たすに過ぎないのだ、と。

　堀川もまた関係性としてのアートを追求した。彼

が送った石は、石というモノであるにもかかわらず、メール・アートに変換することによって、繋がりを安定させる底荷の役割を果たした。

　アポロ11号の石ほどではないにしても、堀川の石はかなりの距離を移動し、生徒たちが石を集めた荒野と東京を物理的につないだ。物質的移動は膨大かつ僅少、東京と信濃川とを繋げつつも地球の構成要素をいささかも変えることはなかった。月面着陸から距離を置いて考えていた堀川は、アームストロングとオルドリンの行為にも似たようなパラドックスを感じていたのだろう。「人類が月に立ち石を持ち帰ったところで宇宙は変りはしない。変わるのは人間であり思考である」とは、作家の言葉である。

　月面から地球へのモノの移動は、宇宙と人間の関係を変えた。もう一つの移動は、人間とその惑星＝地球との関係を変えた。宇宙競争の真っ只中、世界の未来がますます不確定になりつつあった時、堀川は後者が少なくとも前者と同じくらい重要であると挑発的に問題提起した。

（訳・富井玲子）

ジョナサン・キーツは Forbes.com の芸術批評家。

初出：オンライン雑誌『Forbes.com』（2019年3月15日号）掲載（https://www.forbes.com/sites/jonathonkeats/2019/03/15/radicalism-wilderness-japan）。

A Provincial Japanese Artist Bested Neil Armstrong

–

Jonathon Keats

When Neil Armstrong and Buzz Aldrin set foot on the moon, one of their primary tasks was to collect a load of rocks. At precisely the moment of their landing, a Japanese artist named Horikawa Michio led his class of seventh graders along the Shinano River in the Niigata Prefecture, instructing them to help him gather stones. They brought their bounty to the local post office, where Horikawa wrapped the rocks in wire, attached mailing tags, and shipped them to his fellow artists.

Horikawa's *Mail Art by Sending Stones* was a seminal work of Conceptual Art in 1960s Japan, yet it remains virtually unknown in the West. An important new exhibition at the Japan Society in New York (*Radicalism in the Wilderness*) is finally rectifying this oversight, bringing needed attention to the work of Horikawa as well as several other essential 60s conceptualists including Maeyama Tadashi and Matsuzawa Yutaka.

The most prominent of these artists, Matsuzawa made his name by organizing an exhibition with neither artwork nor spectators. Or rather the way in which artists submitted work and the public encountered it fell outside the realm of physical experience. "Please keep your entry in your hand and deliver the formless emission from it to the exhibition site," Matsuzawa wrote in a magazine ad. "Those who wish to enter may start contacting in material and/or immaterial ways."

Given that the exhibition site was in a field far outside of Tokyo, Matsuzawa was undoubtedly shrewd to place minimal physical demands on participants. But *Independent '64 in the Wilderness* was more than just a logistical workaround for an ambitious provincial artist. Even before Western conceptualists such as Sol LeWitt started dematerializing artwork by providing rules for instantiation by others, Matsuzawa revealed that art required only a common point of focus. In essence, art is a relationship between people, objects merely serving as opportune props.

Horikawa also explored art as a relationship. Although the rocks he shipped were objects in their own right, he used them as ballast for connection by transforming them into mail art.

Some stones traveled a considerable distance—if not quite as far as Apollo 11—physically connecting Tokyo with the wilderness where they were collected by his students. The material transfer was simultaneously massive and negligible, connecting the city to the Shinano River while changing nothing about the planet's composition. Standing back, Horikawa perceived an equivalent paradox in the actions of Armstrong and Aldrin. "Nothing has changed in the universe even if humans stand on the moon and bring back moon rocks," he wrote in a statement about his work. "What changes are humans, and their thinking."

One transfer of material altered people's relationship with the universe. The other changed people's relationship with their own planet. In the midst of the Space Race, as the future of the world grew increasingly precarious, Horikawa provocatively proposed that the latter is at least as important as the former.

Jonathon Keats is critic-at-large of Arts for Forbes.com.

Originally published as Jonathon Keats, "See How a Provincial Japanese Artist Bested Neil Armstrong At This Thrilling Japan Society Exhibit," *Forbes.com* (March 15, 2019), https://www.forbes.com/sites/jonathonkeats/2019/03/ 15/radicalism-wilderness-japan.

Review 2
Alex Kitnick

展評 2
アレックス・キトニック

<u>2021.7.4</u>

信濃川で石を採取。その内の 2 個を 7.21 のアポロ 52 周年記念日に郵送する

= I gather stones at the Shinano River. I select two of them and mail them to commemorate the Apollo 11 mission after 52 years.

堀川紀夫の石の作品 ── アース・アートワークが郵便になった時

アレックス・キトニック

1969年、大都市・東京から遠く離れて山岳風景が広がる新潟県で、堀川紀夫は《The Shinano River Plan》を開始した。その実行のために、堀川は日本で一番長い川、信濃川の河川敷で11個の石を採集し、それぞれを針金で巻き、住所、メッセージ、郵便切手を貼付して、何人かの人たちに送った。（自らのコレクションとして、作家は発送する準備の整った石を写真撮影している）。これらの石のいくつかが、2019年の春、ジャパン・ソサエティ開催、富井玲子企画の画期的展覧会「荒野のラディカリズム：グローバル1960年代の日本のアーティスト」での展観のため、はるばるニューヨークにやってきた。

堀川のインスピレーションは、同年のアポロ11号の月面着陸だった。11というアポロ計画のミッション番号をもとに、11個の石を採集することを思いついた。バズ・アルドリンとニール・アームストロングが月面に降り立ち「科学」の名のもとに、天空の石を掴みとった（月面にはどうやら他に持ち帰るものはなかったようだが……）。一方、地球では多くの人びとが宇宙空間に目を凝らしていたが、誰もが同じように見ていたわけではなかった。人によっては、NASAの成果に懐疑的だった。たとえば、前年に亡くなったマーティン・ルーサー・キング・ジュニア牧師の同志、ラルフ・アバナシー牧師は、その遺志をついで貧者の行進をフロリダのケネディ宇宙センター周辺で組織し、アポロの打ち上げに抗議した──政府の財源は冷戦下の米ソの宇宙競争を助長するのではなく、人類の危機を解決すべきだ、と主張して（同じ年、黒人のソウル＋ジャズ詩人のジル・スコット＝ヘロンは、アポロ計画を激しく非難して「男が昨晩私の家賃を値上げした、白んぼが月の上にいるから」と語りによるサウンド作品「月の上の白んぼ」を発表した）。

堀川もまた宇宙競争には慎重だった。というか、より正確には、天空の星にのみ自然の驚異があるとは思っていなかったのだ。堀川にとって地球の石は、月の石と同じくらい魅惑的であり、かつ当たり前でもあった。つまり、人類が天空へと視線を向けたことで、堀川の視線は地球へと下降したのだが、それは堀川一人のことではなかった。たとえば、最初のアー

スデイはその1年後の1970年4月22日にアメリカで始まった。堀川の作品は自然の原初物質を認識し、彫刻の基本素材への回帰を体現している。ただし、「大地に帰る」という懐古の情が作用したわけではない。むしろ、石に新しい方向性を与え、その軌跡を劇的に変えて、石を動員したのだ、とも言える。石礫が飛び交っていた時代である。その前年の1968年、パリでは学生や労働者たちは道路の石畳を剥がして、警察に投げつけていた。堀川の石もまた抗議の石だった。彼は後に、ベトナム反戦を表明するために、日本の佐藤栄作首相とアメリカのリチャード・ニクソン大統領にそれぞれ石を送っている。東京のアメリカ大使館が堀川へ送った見当違いの手紙は、ニクソンが堀川の意図を理解しなかったものの、作品が沈黙の記念碑として機能したことを示す。まさに、追悼の証として世界各地で広く石が墓の上に置かれるように。

堀川の計画（プラン）は、政治的プロジェクトであると同時に美的行為でもあり、当時の現代美術の国際動向に合流する。ランド・アートは、この時期、世界各地で根付きつつあった。1969年、アメリカの作家、ロバート・スミッソンは、コーネル大学付属A・D・ホワイト博物館のアース・アート展に際して、ダンプカー1台分のアスファルトをローマの採石場に流した。そして大学のあるニューヨーク州イサカの現場では、近隣の鉱山で岩塩を採集し、展示場に持ち込んで鏡の破片を王冠のように差し込んだ。また、この展覧会に際して、デニス・オッペンハイムは近くのビーベ湖の水面を覆った氷に切り込み、水路を作った。イタリアでは、アルテ・ポーヴェラ（『貧しい芸術』）周辺の作家たちが現代美術の商業化に抗議して木や石を使った作品を制作した。日本でも「もの派」が大地に関連する物質を素材として検討し始めた。1968年、関根伸夫は巨大な土の円柱を地面から取り出し、《位相－大地》と命名した。堀川自身はグループGUNに所属していて、1970年には雪原に絵具をスプレイすることになる（寒冷な環境で、ジュール・オリツキーの絵画を巨大化した様子、と想像してみたい）。しかし、これらの地上実験の多くは、そのサイト（場）と密接に結びついてい

Horikawa Michio's Stone Work: When Earth Art Hit the Mails*

–

Alex Kitnicks

Horikawa Michio began his *Shinano River Plan* in 1969, in Niigata, Japan, a mountainous landscape far from Tokyo's metropolis. To execute his work, Horikawa collected eleven stones from the banks of the Shinano River—Japan's longest—and wrapped them in wire, which allowed him to affix address, message, and postage, and send his stones to a select group of recipients. (To form his own collection, Horikawa photographed the specimens before shipping them out.) A selection of these objects resurfaced at Japan Society in New York last spring as part of *Radicalism in the Wilderness: Japanese Artists in the Global 1960s*, the groundbreaking exhibition curated by Reiko Tomii.

In 1969, the Apollo 11 spacecraft landed on the moon—the mission's number inspired the artist's selection of eleven samples—and Buzz Aldrin and Neil Armstrong entered a lunar landscape, grabbing celestial stones for science. (Apparently there wasn't much else to take.) Back on Earth, many were wide-eyed for outer space, though not everyone saw it the same way: certain groups remained skeptical of NASA's achievements. Reverend Ralph Abernathy, a close associate of Martin Luther King Jr., organized a Poor People's Campaign march at the Kennedy Space Center in Florida to protest the Apollo launch, arguing that government funds should solve human crises, not foster planetary cold war. (That same year, Gil Scott-Heron lambasted the space program with his spoken-word track "Whitey on the Moon": "The man just upped my rent last night / 'cause Whitey's on the moon.")

Horikawa, too, was wary of the space race, or, perhaps more to the point, he wasn't convinced that wonder resided solely among the stars. The artist found earthly stones just as fascinating, or mundane, as their moonish counterparts. Mankind's turn to the heavens, in other words, brought his gaze down to Earth, and it did so for others as well: the first Earth Day was celebrated a year later, on April 22, 1970. If Horikawa's work represents a recognition of the nature of first things, as well as a return to the most basic of sculptural materials, it did not do so in nostalgic, "back to the land" fashion; rather, the artist mobilized rocks by assigning them new vectors, and dramatically chang-

ing their course. Stones flew at this time. A year earlier, students and workers in Paris had pried cobblestones from the streets and tossed them at police. Horikawa's stones protest, too: he later shipped examples to Prime Minister Sato Eisaku and President Richard Nixon to demonstrate his opposition to the war in Vietnam. The wry note that the U.S. embassy sent to Horikawa suggests that Nixon didn't register the point, but the work serves as a silent memorial all the same: it is custom in many traditions to leave a stone atop a grave as a sign of remembrance.

While Horikawa's *Plan* is part political project, it also constitutes an aesthetic act, and it partakes in wider artistic tendencies of the time. Land art planted itself all over the world at this moment. In 1969, Robert Smithson poured a dump truck's worth of asphalt down a Roman quarry while Cornell University's Andrew Dickson White Museum of Art staged the exhibition *Earth Art*. Here, Smithson imported piles of salt from nearby mines into the gallery, crowning them with mirrors, while Dennis Oppenheim cut a deep channel through the ice covering nearby Beebe Lake. In Italy, artists associated with Arte Povera (literally "poor art") turned to trees and stones to protest commercialization. In Japan, Mono-ha ("School of Things") also began investigations of earthly materials: Nobuo Sekine removed a massive cylinder of dirt from the ground and christened it *Phase—Mother Earth* (1968). Horikawa himself belonged to a group known as GUN, or Group Ultra Niigata, whose activities included spray painting fields of snow (imagine a very large, very cold Jules Olitski). But while so many of these terrestrial experiments bound themselves closely to their sites—one often had to travel great distances, to obscure locales to visit them—Horikawa moved earth in radical ways.

In its emphasis on circulation and distribution, *Shinano River Plan* also belongs to the practice of mail art, a 1960s movement sustained by a network of participants that collapsed distinctions between artist and viewer, sender and receiver. (Significantly, Horikawa also made ersatz stamps parodying the Japanese prime minister.) Ray Johnson presided over the mail scene with his New York Correspondance [*sic*] School,

て、見たい人は往々にして長距離を移動し、その場所を訪れる必要があるのに対して、堀川は大地（の素材）そのものをラディカルに動かした。

　伝達と流通を重視する《The Shinano River Plan》は、メール・アート、つまり1960年代に作家がネットワークを形成し、作家と観客、送信者と受信者の区別を無化した試みの一部でもある（さらに、堀川は総理大臣をパロディ化した偽切手も制作している）。レイ・ジョンソンは、ニューヨーク・コレスポンデンス・スクールの旗印のもとにメール・アートを展開した元祖的存在で、ウサギ風トレードマークをあしらった謎めいたコラージュを無料で世界中の「封筒を舐める者たち」に送った。カナダでは、ジョンソンに触発されたグループのイメージ・バンクが、写真エージェンシーの前身ともいえる機能を果たし、読者の要望に基づいたイメージを集積した。これらの試みは、画廊システムの回避を狙うなど、堀川のメール・アートと共通点も多い。しかしながら、堀川の郵便の活用はイメージではなく物質に重点がある点で異なる。だからこそ、作家は石を梱包するのではなく、可能な限り多くの人々が石に直に触り、さらには石を出発点に考えてほしい、という意図を秘めて、石を単に針金で縛ったオープンな形で郵送したかったのだろう（堀川の石は、「学者の石」とも呼ばれる中国の「供石」のミニマリズム版だろうか）。メール・アートの作家の多くは、美術市場の商品としての作品を皮肉交じりに批判したが、堀川の郵送物には、さらに一種の敵意すら加味されていた。

　堀川のプロジェクトについて言うべきことは数多い。が、題名に示されている「計画」（プラン）という言葉は、とりわけ奇妙*に思える。「計画」の強調は、組織化の強調でもあり、憶測を拒否する。計画という言葉から、私は政治活動やインフラ事業――例えば、スターリンの恐怖の「五ヵ年計画」――を思い浮かべてしまう。堀川は、決定的にDIYで対抗策を考えて、政治やインフラに共通する大規模なスケール感をパロディ化したのかもしれない。にもかかわらず、この言葉には明確な意図と実行が感じられる。堀川は何かを成し遂げようと事を起こしたのだ（この感覚を理解す

るには、同年のロバート・ラウシェンバーグの版画シリーズ《ラリった月**》を考えるとよい。ラウシェンバーグの月面着陸賛歌が、いかに的外れであることか……）。

　しかし、なぜ、今日、堀川の「計画」を美術史ではなく、美術批評の場で論じるのか。ローカルとグローバルの繋がりを主張する堀川の作品は評価すべきであり、ローカルとグローバルの距離を埋めるために、郵便という国家事業を利用した点も重要だ。言い換えるなら、《The Shinano River Plan》が示唆するのは、私たちの足下にある「もの」が遠隔の人びとへと意味を運ぶため、つまり関係の詩学を可能にするためには公の制度が必要だ、ということなのだ。今日、我々が当たり前に思っている美術制度が（一時的であるにせよ？）閉鎖されている、この時に、私たちは何か別の伝達様式を考え始めてもよいのではないか。まさに、今こそ計画を立てる時なのだ。

『4Columns』誌編集者の注：コロナ禍の期間中、美術館や画廊が閉鎖されている状況を踏まえて、手軽にオンラインで閲覧可能で、自分にとって特に意義のある作品について考察するように執筆依頼した。

【訳注】
* キトニックの感じた「奇妙」さは、日本語と英語の違いによるところが大きいだろう。英語では正式に「Apollo Program」あるいは「Project Apollo」と呼ばれているNASAの事業は、日本語では「アポロ計画」と称されていた。今日のように簡単にネット検索できる時代ではなかった。作家は「計画」を英語に訳しなおした「Plan」を作品名に冠している。
** 英語タイトルは《Stoned Moon》で、stonedはドラッグ、特にマリワナでラリった状態をさす。

（訳・富井玲子）

アレックス・キトニックはバード・カレッジアナンデール・オン・ハドソン校の美術史・視覚文化助教授。

初出：オンライン雑誌『4Columns』（2020年6月26日号）掲載（https://4columns.org/kitnick-alex/horikawa-michio）。

sending free, oblique collages, many emblazoned with his signature bunny, to a global constellation of envelope-lickers; in Canada, Image Bank, inspired by Johnson, formed a proto-photo agency, compiling pictures based on their readers' desires. While sharing similar concerns, including the evasion of the gallery system, Horikawa's use of the mail is singular in foregrounding matter over image, which is why it seems important that the artist didn't package his stones but sent them simply wired, out in the open, so as many people as possible might contact—and contemplate—them directly. (Could they be minimalist versions of Chinese *gongshi*, or scholar's stones?) While most mail artists were playfully critical of the commodity, Horikawa's correspondence added a dose of antagonism to boot.

There is much to say about Horikawa's project, but its strange title sticks in mind, especially its emphasis on the plan. The artist refused speculation by stressing organization. The idea of the plan reminds me of political projects and infrastructural undertakings (Stalin's dire Five-Year Plans, for example), and while Horikawa might have been parodying the scale of such endeavors with his decidedly DIY counterplan, the word nevertheless carries a decisive air of intentionality and execution: he set out to accomplish something. (To get a sense of this, compare Horikawa's title to Robert Rauschenberg's bleary-eyed paean to the moon landing, *Stoned Moon*, begun the same year).

But why Horikawa's Plan today, and why discuss it here, not in a scholarly catalog but in a space of criticism? Certainly, Horikawa's insistence on the connection between the local and global is salutary, as is his use of a national service to bridge the gap. Put another way, *Shinano River Plan* declares that the stuff beneath our feet carries meaning for those far away, and that institutions are necessary for making such a poetics of relation possible. In this moment when our traditional art system is (temporarily?) closed, one might begin to consider other modes of address. Now is the time to plan.

* *4Colomns* Editor's Note: In light of the fact that museum and gallery exhibitions remain closed during the coronavirus pandemic, we have invited our contributors to reflect on an artwork that is particularly significant to them and that is easily viewed online.

Alex Kitnick is Assistant Professor of Art History and Visual Culture at Bard College in Annandale-on-Hudson, N.Y.

Originally published as Alex Kitnick, "Horikawa Michio," *4Columns* (June 26, 2020), https://4columns.org/kitnick-alex/horikawa-michio.

Text 1
Reiko Tomii

論考 1
富井玲子

1971.8.13
久しぶりに信濃川に立った。「石を送る」ことをどう収めるかで迷っていた
= I go to the Shinano River after a long while. I have a hard time deciding how to conclude my "stone mailing."

現代美術の地平に石を探る

富井玲子

石の展覧会を考えたことがある。

時期的には1970年前後。同時代の欧米ではアースワークやランド・アートのカテゴリーで考えるところかもしれないが、日本ならランド（大地）やアース（土）ではなく、キーワードは〈石〉だ。

日本の1970年前後といえば、ベトナム反戦・反米運動と連動しつつ大学闘争が激化した1967年から70年にかけて、投石が一種の時代表現ですらあった時代である。ただし、投石の場合には、日常的に私たちがイメージする自然の〈石〉を投げるのではなく、当時の都市風景では当たり前だった舗道の敷石をはがした四角い石（あるいはその砕片）を投げていた。ちなみに、1970年に赤瀬川原平が『朝日ジャーナル』の連載を引き受けたとき、最初に思いついたのは週一で出版される週刊誌の速攻性を生かして、闘争のために全国の敷石情報を流す、というアイディアだったほどだ。

石の展覧会を考えた背景には、石なしには、1970年前後の日本美術史は成立しない、という事実がある。石なしには成立しえないのだが、この時期を考えるとき、石ほどcontentiousな、角の立つものもないのではないか。

なにしろ、1970年前後の石といえば、真っ先に思いつくのが〈もの派〉の石だろう。

李禹煥がガラスと鉄板の上に置いたり、綿の中に埋め込んだり、座布団（?）に載せたり、ゴムの巻尺を引き伸ばして重しにした石もあるし、多摩美グループの関根伸夫、小清水漸や菅木志雄にも石を使った代表作がある。さらには〈もの派〉の周辺に目を移せば、〈幻触〉の小池一誠の切断された石、また河口龍夫の蛍光灯を差し込んだ石もある。

しかし、私の真意は別のところにあった。

私の見せたい石は、コンセプチュアリズムの石だった。それは、従来「概念芸術」として狭く限定された解釈の中でのみ議論されてきた日本のコンセプチュアリズムを、より開かれたグローバルな視点で読み直す作業の一貫であり、このことを私は、1999年クイーンズ美術館での『グローバル・コンセプチュアリズム』展で着手したわけだった。

ここで、私がコンセプチュアリズムと呼ぶものは、従来の美術（絵画彫刻）への問題提起であり、広義のフォーマリズム（美術を色と形に還元する立場）へのクリティークとしてあるのみならず、美術の制度そのものへの批判を重要な契機としてはらむ。そして、作品の自律性を標榜した近代（モダン）的「芸術」観からの離脱をはかる戦略的態度の中にポストモダンの精神的萌芽もふくんでいた、と歴史的に措定できるだろう。だから、アメリカの「概念芸術」の代表選手とみなされているジョーゼフ・コスースは、コンセプチュアリズムのもっとも保守的な例となり、逆に当時の社会運動やプロテストに連動していたアーティストの活動などは、アートを社会へ開かれたものにしようとした点でコンセプチュアリズムに重なってくるものも少なくないのである。

さて、クイーンズ展では、「これは石である」と始まり綿々とトートロジー的に石の認識論を言葉にして書き、その一字一字を石に小穴をあけて嵌め込んだ柏原えつとむの《Rock》を、コンセプチュアリズムの石として出品した。

コンセプチュアリズムの石としてはずせないのは、高松次郎が番号振りをした石も重要だし、コンセプチュアリズムの前形態としてのグループ〈位〉が砂利を画廊に運び込んだ作品も興味深い。絶対にはずせないのは、個人制作の枠を越えた広がりのある作品、堀川紀夫の《石を送るメール・アート》だ。これは、1969年7月21日（日本時間）アポロ11号の月面着陸にちなんで始められたシリーズである。当日、月面着陸と同時刻、堀川は教えていた中学校の生徒を近隣の信濃川の河原に引率して「地球の石」を採取させた。月面での「月の石」採取に呼応するこれらの石から、アポロのミッション番号にちなんで11個の石が選ばれ、郵便局から美術関係者11人に郵送された。このあと、番外篇も含めて、12号、13号（東京ビエンナーレ出品）と連携したメーリングが続き、1972年、アポロ最終号である17号で、堀川の《石を送るメール・アート》も一つの終着点を迎えた。

ところで、この作品について、私が最初に知ったの

Exploring Stones on the Horizon of Contemporary Art

Reiko Tomii

I once thought of curating an exhibition of stones in contemporary art. The time period would be around 1970. Speaking of stones, one may be tempted to organize a show under such Euro-American rubrics as "land art" and "Earthworks." But my aim was to focus on "stones," not "land" (as site) or "earth" (as material), which immediately reminds us of Euro-American examples. But my interest lay in stone-based works from Japan.

In Japan, the year 1970 falls in the period from 1967 to 1970, during which "throwing stones" was a part of the Zeitgeist, with rioting students making it an expression of their rebellion that converged with antiwar and anti-imperialist struggles. However, the "stones" those activists threw were not the round kind found in nature that we ordinarily think of, but the square kind that those protesters ripped up from the paved city streets that formed an everyday urban landscape. So much so, when Akasegawa Genpei accepted an assignment to create a series for the weekly *Asahi Journal*, he initially planned to disseminate up-to-date information on available paved streets. The quick turnaround of weekly publication would have allowed him to spread timely information for activists nationwide.

I thought of an exhibition of stone-based works because the history of Japanese art around 1970 will be incomplete without the study of them. Indeed, the stone was a most contentious material in Japan then, with Mono-ha (School of Things) being top on the list of stone-deploying practitioners.

For example, Lee Ufan used stones in several different ways: he dropped one rock on a glass pane layered over a steel plate, embedded several in cotton, placed one each on a number of cushions, and used some to weigh down stretched rubber tape measures. Among the graduates from Tamabi (abbreviated from Tama Art University), Sekine Nobuo, Koshimizu Susumu, and Suga Kishio also deployed stones in their signature works. Shifting our eye to those around Mono-ha, Koike Kazushige of Genshoku (meaning "Tactile Hallucination") cut stones and Kawaguchi Tatsuo of Group "I" orchestrated a mock insertion of a fluorescent tube through a stone.

However, my intention was elsewhere. Central to my idea were conceptualist stones. By examining them, I wanted to expand the discussion of conceptualism beyond what was long confined to the definition of *Gainen geijutsu*, narrowly and closely defined in line with Euro-American Conceptual Art. This endeavor was what I had started in 1999 with the Japanese section of *Global Conceptualism* at the Queens Museum of Art in New York.

What I call "conceptualism" here constitutes a range of critiques on conventional art practices (painting and sculpture). Not only does it critique formalism in a broader sense (reduction of art to forms and colors), it also calls into question the institution of art itself. Its strategy for transcending the modern construct of Art with a capital A underscored by the autonomy of artworks can be historically understood to prefigure the spirit of the postmodern. Thus, Joseph Kosuth, the representative of American Conceptual Art, embodies the more conservative example of conceptualism, while those engaged in practices linked to social and protest struggles—or containing some degrees of them— may be interpreted as conceptualist in that they aspired to open up art for society.

I presented one conceptualist stone in *Global Conceptualism*: Kashihara Etsutomu's *Rock*, which bears a text that begins by asserting, "This is a stone." This tautological claim is followed by the epistemology of stone, with each character embedded in a small hole bored into the stone.

Among the must-haves in my dream stone exhibition is Takamatsu Jirō's *Stone and Numeral*, in which the artist inscribed a series of numbers onto stones. A fascinating example is *E. Jari* by Group "I," wherein the group brought a huge pile of gravel into a small gallery space. Also indispensable is Horikawa Michio's *Mail Art by Sending Stones*, which generated a network of conceptualist minds. This is a series Horikawa launched in conjunction with the Apollo 11 moon landing on July 21, 1969 (Japanese time). On that day, he brought a class of middle school students to a nearby dry riverbed of the Shinano River and had them gather "earth stones" as the lunar activities were unfolding, which importantly encompassed the gathering of moon rocks.

はクイーンズ展の調査の時だった。彦坂尚嘉から堀川の石を教えられ、また後に彼が雑誌『アクリラート』（1997年）で堀川にインタビューした記事を読んだ。それを読んだとたん、石を郵送するというコンセプトの面白さと、歴史・社会的なコンテクストを包含する作品の広がりに瞠目した。が、いかんせん、その時点では、クイーンズ展の作品選択は終了しており、理論的な展覧会構成の中に、取り込むにはいささか無理があった。何と言っても、同展は、私のコンセプチュアリズム論の基礎骨格を初めて歴史化したものだったから……。

しかし、堀川の石を紹介する機会は時を経ずして訪れた。『グローバル・コンセプチュアリズム』展をきっかけに、同工異曲で20世紀の「都市」という場に生まれた美術と文化を地球規模で考えるテート・モダンの『センチュリー・シティー』展に企画参加することになったからだ。

1970年前後の東京をテーマとして参加した『センチュリー・シティー』展（2001年）については、同人誌『テオリア』第1−7号（2001−2年）に執筆したので繰り返さない（本稿は7号掲載のテキストを大幅に改訂したものである）。

テート・モダン展の話があったとき、クイーンズ展の延長としてコンセプチュアリズム関係では是非とも堀川紀夫の《石を送るメール・アート》を紹介したいと考えた。日本の60年代美術は作品の現存しない例が少なくないが、さいわいなことに、アポロ12号の際に東京画廊主・山本孝と美術評論家・瀧口修造に送った石が荷札も完全に現存していた（それぞれ、現在は田畑幸人氏と富山県立近代美術館の所蔵）。展覧会直前、真珠湾攻撃の日とミレニアム元旦にテート館長へ発送された新しい石2点を加えて、展観に付すことができた。また、石の写真や郵便局の領収証などの資料を貼りこんだり、宛先をリストした記録シートも一部壁に展示した。

堀川の石を出すとして、〈1970年前後の東京〉セクションでは何らかの形で〈もの派〉を扱わざるを得ない。石に限って考えるなら、企画のオプションとして

は二通りある。〈もの派〉の石を出す、あるいは出さない。これは、私の〈もの派〉観にかかわる選択である。

〈もの派〉の歴史的な核は関根伸夫の作品と李禹煥の言説に集約されるとするのが私の立場だから、東京画廊で1969年に発表された《空相−油土》の写真と、それについて書いた李禹煥の関根論をパネル展示し、ものの作品もいくつか見せる、というのが私の構想だった。李禹煥は1972年に始まった《線より》のシリーズで代表させて絵画を出品し、あえて石は出さなかった。つまり、1970年前後の石を堀川のメール・アートの石で代表させたのである。

この時期の美術における石の定番（あるいは定石！）は、もの派の石——より正確には、李禹煥の《関係項》と題された一群の石の作品だろう。それがこれまで書かれてきた美術史における常識的な選択であり、テート・モダン側から、たとえば石と綿を組み合わせた李作品を出せないか、というような打診が企画の過程にあったことも事実である。

もしも、10都市＝セクションの一つではなく、〈1970年前後の東京〉だけの展覧会で、それなりのスペースが会場にもカタログにも確保できるのであれば〈もの派〉の石も入っているべきところだった。

なぜなら、堀川の石は、当時李禹煥が批判した石であり、批評的に考えても美術史的に考えても、批判した側と批判された側を、同じ〈石〉の一点で突き合わせてみるのは意味のあることだからだ。蛇足になるが、言うまでもなく、それが石の展覧会を考えた一つの理由である。

突き合わせるとして、石をもののレベルで比べることも可能だし、展覧会というフィジカルな場は、そうした作業に有効だ。しかし、それは将来の機会にゆずるとして、ここでは石を言葉のレベルで考えてみたい。

堀川の石を批判した李のテキストは、『美術手帖』69年11月号掲載、「観念の芸術は可能か——オブジェ思想の正体とゆくえ」と題されたもの。10頁（pp.70−79）にわたる文章の冒頭に唯一図版掲載されていたの

Based on the Apollo's mission number, he selected eleven stones and mailed them out from a post office to eleven people in the art world. Subsequently, he mailed stones, both in conjunction with Apollo 12 and 13 (the latter of which coincided with *1970 Tokyo Biennale*) and on non-Apollo occasions. His series culminated with the mailing that coincided with the final Apollo 17 mission in 1972.

I first learned of Horikawa's mail art during my research for *Global Conceptualism*. One of the artists intended for the Japanese section, Hikosaka Naoyoshi told me about Horikawa; he was familiar with the Niigata artist's work because he conducted and published an interview with Horikawa in the art journal *Acrylart* in 1997. Upon reading the interview, I was captivated by Horikawa's marvelous idea of mailing stones and the social and historical dimension engendered by them. Alas, by then, the selection for the Japanese section was complete. At that late stage, it was not easy to add his work into the theoretical framework I narrowly devised as the first step of historicizing conceptualism in Japan.

However, an opportunity soon materialized to present Horikawa's stones, as my participation in *Global Conceptualism* led to another global exhibition, *Century City* at Tate Modern in London in 2001. The focus was given to "flashpoint" moments in ten 20th-century cities when modern art and culture arose in a significant manner.

My curatorial focus was "Tokyo, ca. 1970" (1967–1973), of which I wrote extensively in Japanese in the journal *Theoria* (nos. 1–7, 2001–2). This text has been substantially revised from its final installment.

When I was invited to curate a Japanese section of *Century City*, I thought of extending my endeavor in *Global Conceptualism* by including Horikawa's *Mail Art by Sending Stones*, as well as adopting a more multidisciplinary selection, including underground theater and photography among other media.

Although many vanguard works from 1960s Japan are no longer extant, some of Horikawa's stones were then known to exist in a relatively good condition, including ones from *The Shinano River Plan: 12* (sent in conjunction with the Apollo 12 mission) mailed to

Yamamoto Takashi, the owner of Tokyo Gallery, and Takiguchi Shūzō, an eminent art critic (now respectively in the collection of Tabata Yukihito and Toyama Prefectural Museum of Art and Design). Prior to the exhibition opening, Horikawa sent two new stones, one each on Pearl Harbor Day and New Year's day, the latter to mark the new millennium, to Tate Gallery's director. In addition to these four stones were a selection of data cards with which the artist documented his mailings by collating mailing data, photographs, and receipts, among other elements.

Aside from Horikawa's stones, my "Tokyo, ca. 1970" section would be incomplete without Mono-ha. I had the curatorial option of whether or not to show stones by Mono-ha. The decision concerned my historical understanding of Mono-ha.

The history of Mono-ha in essence centers on Sekine Nobuo's work and Lee Ufan's discourse. My plan was to show a photograph of Sekine's *Phase of Nothingness—Oilclay*, which he showed at Tokyo Gallery in 1969, and Lee's text on this work, both to be presented as panels. Lee's work could be represented by *From Line*, his painting series begun in 1972 (one work was in Tate Modern's collection). In other words, no stones of Lee or Mono-ha. I let Horikawa's stones stand in for the whole of Japanese engagement with stone around 1970.

In a conventional view, the definitive works involving stones include none other than Mono-ha's—more precisely Lee Ufan's series *Relatum*, which encompasses his above described works. This would have been a more standard choice based on the by-then established narrative. Indeed, Tate Modern's curators asked me if I was (also) interested in showing Lee's sculpture, say, stones imbedded in cotton.

If it were a stand-alone exhibition, not one out of ten sections, with ample space for both the display and the publication, Mono-ha's, especially Lee's, stones would have been indispensable to examine "Tokyo ca. 1970."

Horikawa's stones were anti-Mono-ha, at least in the eye of Lee Ufan who criticized it. It will be meaningful, both art critically and art historically, to compare the works by an artist who made a critique and

が、堀川の石だった（なお、この石は堀川のデータシートによれば、李禹煥に直接送られた石ではなく、同誌編集長の宮澤壯佳に送られたものだ。この掲載の後、69年11月のアポロ12号に関連して、堀川は李に石を送っている）。

反オブジェ論として書かれたテキストは、冒頭で堀川の石を「ただの『石』であり、それ以上でもそれ以下でもない、『定められた石』であるに過ぎない」(p.70)と批判した後、高松次郎が河原の石にペンキで数字を書いたイベントを「石は『石』にされ、作家によって作り変えられた『作品』としての虚像性を発するように措定された」と切り返し、続いてプロセス・アートや、アースワーク、コンセプチュアル・アートなどポストミニマリズム的作品群を「反芸術」として横断的に弾劾する。後半には、この時期の李らしく、ゼードルマイヤー、フランカステル、ヘーゲル、マルクーゼなどを引きながら、近代美術の様相を説き、その上で、ポップに「表象作用の完璧性」を認め、ミニマルに「観念と物体の分離」を言い、現状の「コンセプチュアリズム」に「行くところを失った観念がその末路において、いかに不安定な浮遊を続けているか」と観察する。無論、現状に完全否定なのではなくて、文末では関根伸夫等の仕事の意義へと落し込んでいく、李らしい文章構成である。69年当時には〈もの派〉という言葉すらなかったわけだが、〈もの派〉を掲げずして実質的に〈もの派〉を擁護するテキストの一つになっている。

このテキストは、日本でも欧米でも当時ほとんど使われなかった「コンセプチュアリズム」という言葉が美術批評で使われたほとんど一番早い例の一つではないか。もっとも、李の定義は私の定義とは異なり「観念の自立、そのための意識の全面的な開発に乗り出そうとしている」点を鑑みての所謂である (p.73)。コンセプチュアリズムとは何かを美術史的に考えるにあたって、格好の対比点となる。

硬い理論的批判はさて置いて、李の〈もの派〉理論における「あるがままの世界」「仕草」「出会い」などに対応するような、より李らしいフレーズから、そのオブジェ批判を拾ってみよう。そこに、李本来の認識の

感性が看取されると私は考えるからである。

高松の石ころは「己れの表情と言葉を押さえられ、『把えられた対象』、つまりは作家の表象物として虚像と化せられる」(p.70)。コスースの言語作品に「標された言葉は、言葉自身の世界を語らず、作家の意図する観念の凝固語に変造されてしまったオブジェ」、ジョーンズの旗は「虚像の実体化として出来上がった作品、すなわち表象したい観念を対象へと凝固させたもの」であり (p.72)、アースワークなどで「そこに提示されている『作品』は、ちょうど作家の意図した観念そのもの以外のなにものでもなく、それが、それ以上それ以外の世界を語ってはくれない」(p.77)、などなど。

ここで、決定的に思えるのは、西洋近代に対してカウンターモダニズムを標榜する論法が、近代哲学の意味空間を前提に成立していることではないだろうか。つまり、主体と対象の固定・静止した抽象的な認識関係を前提にしているのである。

しかし、李が批判する表現は、そうした自律空間での意味作用が破綻した、それを破綻させたところから始まるのではないか。しかし、李は「像の対象化」にオブジェ（レディメード）が用いられ、オブジェ「自体がそもそも虚像」であり、また「虚像の実体化」だとする。一方、私の考えるモダニズム以降の基礎戦略たるコンセプチュアリズムにおいて、オブジェは現実世界の実体である。それは実像であるが、自己完結するモノではなく、社会・文化・歴史などのマトリックスの核となり、（フーコー流と言ってもよいが）縦横に網目を作り出しうるものとして、「この現実世界」に存在するのである。

一つ断っておくが、こうした私の視点が、ポストモダンを通過してモダンを相対化した後知恵であると認めることはやぶさかではない。また、コンセプチュアリズムを概念 (concept) あるいは観念 (idea) の芸術とのみ規定せず、近代批判の戦略性としてグローバルに考える立場も、欧米でコンセプチュアル・アートが顕著になった60年代から数十年の時間をへた目があるから再考しうることも事実である。だから、わたしの

an artist who received it on the single shared element of "stones." Needless to say, that was precisely the reason why I thought of the aforementioned exhibition of stones, to begin with.

Comparison can be made on a few levels. A physical level concerns "stones" as things. An exhibition is an ideal site to undertake such an object-based comparison. Or, comparison can be done on a discursive level, as will be outlined below.

Lee critiqued Horikawa's stone in his essay "Is an Art of *Kannen* Possible? The Truth and Future of the *Objet* Thought" in the November 1969 issue of *Bijutsu techō*. The only illustration to this essay was Horikawa's stone and the text began with it. (According to his data sheet, this stone was not sent to Lee himself, but to the magazine's chief editor Miyazawa Take-yoshi; after this publication, Horikawa sent a stone to Lee in conjunction with the Apollo 12 mission.)

Lee's essay is his argument against *objets*—which as a Japanese art term means Duchampian Readymades and works incorporating them—and the thinking that underscores such *objets*-based work. He faulted Horikawa's stone as "a mere 'stone,' nothing more or nothing less, just a 'predetermined stone'" (p. 70). This indictment is followed by that of Takamatsu Jirō's *Stone and Numeral*, for which Lee claims that the artist "turned a stone into 'stone,' recast as a 'work of art' imbued with a sense of illusion." Lee went on with his critique on a wide range of post-minimalism including process art, land art, and conceptualism, indicting them as "anti-art." In the latter half of the essay, Lee explicates the state of modern art in reference to Sedlmayr, Francastel, Hegel, and Marcuse among others; and acknowledges a "perfection of representation" in Pop, a "separation of ideas and things" in minimalism, and an "insecure floating of ideas that lost their directions and are in the dire final state" in conceptualism. Among precious few that escaped his criticism was Sekine Nobuo's work. This exemplifies a typical writing strategy of Lee's at the time. Granted, there was no such word as "Mono-ha" in 1969; still, without using the very term, he was establishing his Mono-ha discourse against the background of what he deemed was lacking in contemporary art.

Notably, he used the term "conceptualism," which was not in frequent use either in Japan or Euro-America at the time. Although his was among its earliest uses, Lee used it to mean "the autonomy of ideas, and an effort to make a full development of consciousness for that," making an intriguing counterpoint to consider the definition of conceptualism.

Setting aside this terminology of Lee's, we can probe Lee's argument against *objets* thinking in his typical phraseologies such as "the world as it is" (*aruga mama no sekai*), "act" (*shigusa*), and "encounter" (*deai*), which taken together reveal the core essence of Lee's epistemology.

According to Lee, Takamatsu's stones are "turned into an illusion, for it is 'comprehended as an object,' that is the artist's representation, when their appearance and language are suppressed" (p. 70). In Kosuth's language work, "language given in them does not narrate its world; instead, it is distorted as a congelation of the idea intended by the artist." Likewise, Johns's flag is "a materialization of an illusion, that is, an idea which the artist desires to represent congeals into an object" (p. 72). Furthermore, in Earthworks, "a 'work' presented therein is nothing but the idea intended by the artist, narrating no world other than itself" (p. 77).

Crucially, Lee's logic of countering Western modernism is predicated upon the signification of modern philosophy. That is to say, his logic is predicated upon the fixed, static, abstract cognitive relationship between subject and object. Still, it appears to me that the works that Lee criticizes in fact emerge precisely where the signification in such an autonomous space has collapsed or is collapsed. Nonetheless, Lee insists that *objets* (Readymades) are used for "representation," that *objets* "themselves are illusions," or "materialized illusions."

In contrast, conceptualism as I understand is the foundational strategy to transcend modernism. With this definition of conceptualism, *objets* are entities in real life; they remain real images yet they are never self-contained because they constitute the node in a socio-cultural and historical web, engendering Foucaultian networks to exist in "this real world."

李禹煥読解の趣旨は、その思考の時代性を明らかにすることではあれ、言葉尻をとらえてあげつらうことにはない。〈もの派〉をめぐる言説がcontentiousだからこそ、時間という距離を意識することは重要なのだ。無論のこと、かくいう私の思考もまた時代性の中にあり、何年かの後に乗り越えられていくであろうことも私は覚悟している（『テオリア』7号での私の否定的な李禹煥解釈に作家本人から疑問が呈されたが、現在では堀川の石を評価している、というコメントがあったことをも付言しておきたい）。

　論を進めよう。グローバルな近代批判の戦略性としてコンセプチュアリズムを考えると、オブジェは形而上学的な抽象物ではない。むしろ、一種の仕掛け、装置 (apparatus) ——多くの場合は、そこから作家の意図やコントロールすらこえた数多の言説を紡ぎ出し、促す装置——として機能する。

　すぐれたオブジェ作品の場合には、作品はそれらしき実体をすら必要としない。たとえば、究極のオブジェ、元祖デュシャンの《泉》は、一介の小便器が展覧会に出品され、拒否されたものだ。が、それは仏陀に比して芸術写真としてスティーグリッツに撮影され、『ブラインドマン』という同人誌にデュシャンの声明文と共に図版掲載され、実体が失われてもなお言説として残った。以後、オリジナルの実体を失った《泉》について発せられた言葉の量を考えてもみてほしい。実に眩暈がするではないか。しかも戦後のデュシャン再評価の波に乗り、精巧なレプリカが作家監督下にエディション制作され、それが美術館に入り、オークションに出され、改めてモノによる美術史のカノンに再編されて大団円を閉じてしまいすらした。

　日本版では、赤瀬川原平の模型千円札が、これに匹敵する優れものであるが、デュシャンのレディメードについての私見とともに「『日常性への下降』から『芸術性への上昇』へ」として論じたものが『うごくモノ——「美術品」の価値形成とは何か』（平凡社　2004年刊）に収録されている。

　コンセプチュアリズムにおいて、作品は、李が近代主義として忌避した「つくること」でもなく、あるいは関根伸夫がこだわったその反対の「つくらないこと」に回避するものでもなく、言わば「組織」するものである。

　堀川の石に戻ると、メール・アートの石は回を重ねるにしたがい、その組織化が進んでいく。稲憲一郎らの《精神衛生研究所》に記録されているように、ニクソン大統領に送られることでベトナム反戦の石となり、後に「地球の石」という荷札がつけられるなど、言説装置としての精度が上がっていく。また、作品としての仕掛けも入念で、最初からデータシートを作成して、石の宛先や重量、総量の記載や写真記録、さらには作品受取の関連資料なども保存している。このレベルでの充実は作品の幅を広げるものであり、それ自体資料ではなく「作品」であり、その位置付けでテート展に若干出品した。言説の広がりという点では、当時「おもしろい先生」として新聞記事になったことは、また作品の重要な一部である。このことは、テートの館長宛に送られた新作の石を秘書が手元にとどめ、なかなか展示課に回したがらなかった、というエピソードにもその人気のほどがあらわれている。

　こうして、石は「それ以上でもそれ以下でもない」どころか、事物の外側へと、雄弁に世界を開示していくものとして、世界に回路を開いていく契機として提示されるのである。

　こう考えていくと、李理論における「開かれた世界」「あるがままの世界」とは何だったのか、という疑問があらためて浮かんでくるだろう。

　図式的に整理するなら、李のいう〈世界〉は知覚のみならず、それを包含する認識の世界であり、〈もの派〉理論は近代を終える動向の中ですぐれて認識論的なものだったと考えられる。近代を終えるとあえて書くのは、〈もの派〉作品がモダニズムの自律空間をそのハビタット（生息地）として、そこに自足する傾向が強いからだ。一方で、コンセプチュアリズムの〈世界〉は現実の世界であり、主体の積極的な関与が志向していく空間である。言い換えれば、作品が即物的にモダニズムの自律空間（たとえば美術館のホワイトキュー

My viewpoint is definitely retrospective, one that reevaluates modernism through the eye that experienced postmodernism. Furthermore, the benefit of hindsight is undeniable in my understanding of conceptualism, which departs from the conventional definition centering on "concept" or "idea," prevalent in and after the 1960s. Instead, from a global perspective of the late 20th century, I define it as diverse strategies in critique of the modern. Hence, my goal of reading Lee Ufan today is to contextualize his thinking against the background of the 1960s and 70s. All the more because the Mono-ha discourse was contentious at the time, it is beneficial to reexamine it now afresh. Yet, I must admit that my standing, too, is constrained by the time in which I live and may be superseded in the future. (I would like to add here that when an earlier version of this essay was published in *Theoria*, no. 7, Lee questioned my interpretation, while acknowledging the more positive appraisal he came to have about Horikawa's stones. Since then, I have added a more historical nuance to my reading.)

In conceptualism, understood as a global set of strategies for modernity critique, an *objet* is no metaphysical abstraction. Rather, it functions as a kind of apparatus often generative of discourses that go beyond its creator's intention and even control.

The value of an *objet* can be irrespective of its material presence. For example, Duchamp's *Fountain*, the ultimate *objet* in art history, was a urinal presented to and rejected from an exhibition. Following this incident, Stieglitz photographed it, comparing it to a Buddha statue, published in the coterie magazine *Blindman* together with Duchamp's statement. It hence survived the loss of its material body in the form of discourse. Since then, a mind-boggling number of words has been uttered to interpret this enigma. In the postwar decades, as Duchamp's oeuvre was reexamined, its replicas were made with precision under the supervision of the artist himself. They thus gained commodity status, entering museum collections, auctioned off, and solidly accepted into the canon of art history.

In Japan, Akasegawa Genpei's *Model 1,000-Yen Note* has achieved a comparable discursive and com-

modity status. (See my article, "State v. (Anti-)Art: *Model 1,000-Yen Note Incident* by Akasegawa Genpei and Company," *positions 10*, no. 1 [2002]: 141–72.)

Unlike Lee who abhorred "making" as part of modernism or Sekine who insisted on "not making" as its antidote, conceptualism encourages to "organize."

In the case of Horikawa, his organizational scheme evolved as he continued with his *Mail Art by Sending Stones*. As documented in *Psychophysiology Research Institute*, he sent a stone to President Nixon. In doing so, this stone represented his protest against the Vietnam War. He later added a tag saying "stone of the earth" to emphasize the point. His stone mailing thus grew in its discursive capacity. From the beginning, its material organization was well thought out, with all the related information recorded on the data cards. The accumulated data encompass addressees, each stone's weight, and photographic documents, along with receipts sent from some addresses. They constitute his "work" as such, rather than being mere documents; that is why I included some data cards in *Century City*. The discursive space his stone generated presents a populist dimension, as the stone works made by an "thought-provoking art teacher" became a topic of newspaper reports. The popularity of his stones is such that when the stone was sent to the director of Tate Gallery, his assistant wanted to keep it at her desk as long as possible before handing it over to the museum's exhibition division.

Far from being "mere" stones, "nothing more or nothing less," Horikawa's stones open themselves up and eloquently reveal the working of the external world. In other words, they function as an apparatus of engendering a circuit of communication.

If so, we may ask once again: What was the "open world" or "world as it is" in Lee's theory?

Simply put, Lee's "world" is a world not only of perception but also of cognition. His Mono-ha theory was highly epistemological among the attempts to end modernism. I just wrote "end modernism" because Mono-ha works make the modernist autonomous space their habitat and tend to linger there. In contrast, the world of conceptualism is the real world toward which the subject's agency is proactively engaged. That is to say, even

初出：富井玲子『現代美術の地平に石を探る　堀川紀夫の《石のメール・アート》』(BAKU 出版局　2012 年)

ブ）の中で展示される場合にも、その圏外に作品の意味の所在を作り出すベクトルが認められる。これは、近代を終えるだけではなく、近代を越える動きとしてとらえられるのではないか？　そして、これが現在につながってくるコンセプチュアリズムの意義であり、堀川の石の意義でもある。

　注意すべきなのは、ここまで私が無定義に使ってきた近代と近代主義、およびそれに対応するカタカナのモダンとモダニズムという概念は、西欧起源の普遍的概念を前提としてきた。これは、李の理論でも、当時の日本の思想文化状況でも暗黙の前提として機能している。実際には、日本における〈近代〉と〈現代〉という二項対立を読み解いていかなければ、60年代に〈現代美術〉として定着した近代の日本的外延を理解し得ないのであるが、そのためには稿を改めねばならない。だが、一言しておくならば、批評家・宮川淳が言説化した〈現代〉の概念を李禹煥は継承しているのであり、〈近代〉と〈現代〉が錯綜する中で〈現代美術〉が本来〈近代〉の装置である〈美術館〉を勝ち取ることにより自らを正当化していく中で、〈もの派〉の作品や理論は中心的な位置を占めたことである。

　このナラティブとは接点を持ちつつも、ほぼ無関係に堀川の石は存在していた。だからこそ、作家が世界との関わり（堀川のいう「作品行為の意味」）を見失ったときに《石を送るメール・アート》は一度終焉せざるを得なかったわけだが、21世紀を迎えて世界（意味）を再発見することで、《石を送るメール・アート》は再制作ではなく〈再開〉が可能になったのだ。（私がテート・モダン展のためにまた《石を送るメール・アート》を美術館に送ることができるかを打診したところ、「それをする意味が見つかれば」という返事が返ってきたことを私は鮮明に覚えている。）

　そして、美術史家としての私の役割は、現代美術のナラティブを再考、拡充しつつ、堀川の《石を送るメール・アート》のストーリーを織り込むことにある。いや、より正確には、堀川がメール作品の石を時として川原に返したように、堀川の石を現代美術の地平に取り返すことだ、というべきかもしれない。

when the work is physically displayed in the modernist autonomous space (such as the white cube of a museum), it reveals a direction to generate signification outside that space. This exemplifies a movement that not just ends modernism but transcends (or moves beyond) it. This is the theoretical implication of conceptualism that extends to today, as much as that of Horikawa's *Stones*.

Notably, modernity or modernism discussed here are predicated on the universalism originated in the West. The same applies to Lee's theory, as well as the cultural milieu of 1960s Japan. Yet, without introducing the concept of *kindai* (modern) and *gendai* (contemporary) to our study, we cannot begin to comprehend the situation of 1960s Japan, wherein *gendai bijutsu*, literally "contemporary art" was established. But this goes beyond the scope of this essay. Suffice it to say that Lee inherited the concept of *gendai* articulated by the critic Miyakawa Atsushi. When *kindai* and *gendai* co-existed without being clearly separated, Mono-ha occupied the central place in the mainstreaming of *gendai bijutsu* as it legitimized itself by winning the space of the museum that is quintessentially modern.

Horikawa's stones existed only cursorily associated with this narrative. That is why *Mail Art by Sending Stones* had to end, when the artist lost his contact with this world, provided by the Apollo missions. (Or, he lost the "meaning of the work" in his own words.) That is why he could resume the series (as opposed to "recreate" the series) in the beginning of the 21st century, when he rediscovered the world (the meaning). I clearly remember the answer he gave me when I asked him whether he might send stones to the museum for the Tate Modern exhibition: "I will, if I can find a meaning to do so."

My role as an art historian, then, is to reexamine and expand the narrative of contemporary art, while weaving the story of Horikawa's *Mail Art by Sending Stones* into it. More precisely, not unlike Horikawa who sometimes returned stones he had gathered for his mail art to the river, I will revive his stones to the horizon of contemporary art.

(Translated from the Japanese original by the author)

Originally published as Reiko Tomii, *Gendai bijutsu no chihei ni ishi o saguru: Horikawa Michio no ishi mēru āto* [Exploring stones on the horizon of contemporary art: Horikawa Michio's Mail Art by Sending Stones] (Jōetsu: Baku Shuppan-kyoku, 2012).

No.8

領　収　証　　No._____

〒949-86
十日町市中条旭町・樋口方
堀　川　紀　夫　様　　44年11月44日
TEL(2)2034

伍百弗也

但　石切代

上記正に領収いたしました
45年5月10日
中原佑介
新潟県十日町市大字高山乙541の1
株式会社 池田石材工業
電②2988番 有線41612番

TITLE
NAME
DATE

中原佑介より《The Shinano River Plan: 12》のレシートにサインをいただく
= Nakahara Yūsuke signs the receipt of *The Shinano River Plan: 12*.

行為と情報：GUN と堀川紀夫をめぐって

富井玲子

はじめに

さる3月8日にニューヨークのジャパン・ソサエティで「荒野のラジカリズム──グローバル1960年代の日本の現代美術家たち」がオープンした。2016年に出版された拙著『荒野のラジカリズム──国際的同時性と日本の1960年代美術』（MIT大学出版局）を展覧会に仕立てたものだ。

ただし、書物はそのままでは展覧会になりえない。展覧会はモノによる議論である。著作では、全体として世界美術史構築の方法論提示を目論んだが、その構築要素である松澤宥、GUN、ザ・プレイの三者については、それぞれの出自から説き起こす作家論的な論述を目指した。が、〈物質消滅〉をテーゼにした松澤のみならず、GUNもザ・プレイもうっかりすると〈作品〉ではなく〈資料〉と片付けられかねないモノ、モノにすらならない行為を残したコンセプチュアリズムの作家達である。

そうした作品をモノとして読み直し、展覧会を作りこむ必要があった。

このことは、私の作家理解、作品理解を一歩も二歩も前進させる結果となった。さらにGUNは二人の中心メンバー、堀川紀夫と前山忠が展覧会のオープンに来米、報道関係者とのインタビューや、関連プログラム「作家との対話」を通じて、改めて生の声を聞けたのも収穫だった。

一番大きな発見は、行為、あるいはパフォーマンス・アートを情報から読み直す、そして誰が情報の主体かを考える、という視点だった。

パフォーマンス研究の困難は、行為の本質が現場性と現時性にある──つまり、行為はその場、その時に実践されて、事実上消えてしまう、ephemeralだ、という点にある。だから、どうしても〈記録〉に頼らざるを得ない。

近代に成立した制度としての美術史は、絵画・彫刻なる自律的（autonomous）かつ即自的（self-sufficient）なモノを対象として成立、展開してきた。それに準じて、モノの残らない行為をベースとしたパフォーマンス・アートを、〈写真〉という〈準・絵画〉──つまり、時空の四次元に生起した行為を二次元のイメージで記録するモノ──を手がかりに記述してきた。この経緯で、〈写真〉は記録物として扱われ、多くの場合〈作品〉ならぬ二義的〈資料〉と見なされることになった。

ひとまず、このようにパフォーマンス・アートの研究史を要約できるだろう。

私は、資料≠作品、という構図に長く疑問を持っていた。平田実や羽永光利のように、ハイレッド・センターやゼロ次元と、いわば共犯者として、あるいは目撃者として共生した写真家を考えると、行為の記録写真だからと言って〈資料〉に過ぎない、とする見方は、写真家の現場へのコミットメントへの理解が欠けるように思えたからだ。

さらに、まだまだ現代美術の市場が黎明期だった日本の60年代には、篠原有司男が提唱したように、〈芸術の無償性〉神話を乗り越えて、〈パブリシティ〉による有償性を現代のマスメディアに求める戦略は、作家のみのオペレーションでは叶わない部分も多々あり、ジャーナリズムに通じていた平　田や羽永のような存在は不可欠だったとさえ言える。この点では、近代的な著者・作者の唯一性を前提にした議論では限界がある。むしろ、協働性を視野に入れた議論が求められる。

だからこそ、作家の行為が先行する、と認めた上で、写真家の写真がそれ自体として写真家の〈作品〉であると同時に、作家の行為の〈作品〉に「第二の人生」を付与するものとして理解することを提案した。[1]

情報は、記録写真（さらには記録動画）だけではなく、堀川紀夫の《石を送るメール・アート》のデータカードや、ザ・プレイにおけるポスターなどのグラフィック作品や報告類など文書もあり、やはりこれらは〈資料〉という概念で処理されている。いずれも、〈行為〉を、自己完結するモノとしての絵画・彫刻と同一平面上に並べて表現の唯一の表出とみなし、行為にまつわる情報の総体＋作品とする前提がある。

そもそもは、作品が自己完結すると措定する近代的作品概念自体が問題にされねばならないのだが、そのためには美術史の方法論として作品概念を解体する

Act and Information: A Reflection on GUN and Horikawa Michio

—

Reiko Tomii

Introduction

—

On March 8, 2019, *Radicalism in the Wilderness: Japanese Artists in the Global 1960s* opened at Japan Society in New York. The exhibition was based on my book, *Radicalism in the Wilderness: International Contemporaneity and 1960s Art in Japan*, published by MIT Press in 2016.

A book in itself rarely makes an exhibition. The exhibition is an object-based proposition. In the book, I aimed to outline a methodology of world art history while presenting detailed accounts of three protagonists—Matsuzawa Yutaka, The Play, and GUN—from their respective origin points. One characteristic shared by these practitioners is the ephemerality of their conceptualism. A stanch immaterialist, Matsuzawa embraces the notion of "Vanishing of Matter." The Play and GUN were performatively oriented collectives. They all left what is often regarded as paper-based "documents" rather than object-based "works of art."

To mount an exhibition of these three, I needed to reexamine their works as objects to display. This preparation helped me to advance my understanding of these artists and their works tremendously. Especially with GUN, two lead members, Horikawa Michio and Maeyama Tadashi, came to New York for the opening. Through their media interviews, related talk programs, and exhibition walk-throughs, I was able to deepen my view on their works.

The biggest discovery was an analytic to consider their performative acts through information management and to reassess their agency of generating and disseminating information. The difficulty of performance study lies in the inescapable fact that the act exists in "now" and "here" fleetingly. That is, it is ephemeral. The study of performance art inevitably relies on its "record." The discipline of art history evolved in modern times as studies of painting and sculpture as autonomous and self-sufficient objects. Accordingly, performance art that leaves scant objects behind has been studied through "photography" which is "quasi painting," turning the four-dimensional act into two-dimensional imagery. In this process, photographs are frequently treated as mere "records," secondary to a "work" as such. Simplistic as it may sound, this has been the nature of performance study in art history.

I have long questioned the distinction between "work" (*sakuhin*) and "document" (*shiryō*). Take, for example, such photographers as Hirata Minoru and Hanaga Mitsutoshi, who avidly photographed the performative works by such collectives as Hi Red Center and Zero Jigen (Zero Dimension). These photographers formed a symbiotic relationship with their subjects-artists, with the former serving at once as witnesses and co-conspirators for the latter. If we regard their photographs as "mere documents," we lose sight of their commitments to the artists reveling in the on-site, in-the-moment acts.

In 1960s Japan, where the market for contemporary art was at best nascent, publicity was another local factor in the artists-photographers equation. As famously proposed by Shinohara Ushio, some artists sought their reward in the mass media, rejecting the myth of "art as reward-less act" (*geijutsu no mushōsei*), the Japanese formulation of "art for art's sake." Still, artists needed a non-art solution to operate in the media sphere. The vacuum was filled by such photojournalists as Hanaga and Hirata (who saw both social news value and cultural merit especially in the street performances). In this sense, the collaboration with photographers was an operational necessity for artists. Hence, a different narrative tangent is required for our discussion.

That is why I have proposed the following. We must acknowledge these photographs of performance art as the "work" of photographers and resituate them as the "second life" of the performative "work" of the artist.[1] It should be noted that photographic records (or moving-image records) are not the only kind of information to document a performative work. Information can also be found in Horikawa Michio's data cards in *Mail Art by Sending Stones* and The Play's graphic works (e.g., posters) and documents (i.e., reports), which have also been traditionally regarded as "documents" (*shiryō*). The logic to deny the status of "work" for these kinds of information lies in the tendency to treat "act" similarly to "painting" and "sculpture" equipped with self-sufficient objecthood.

のみならず、近代的装置としての美術館がモノとしての作品を収集展観する場所として機能する事実にも配慮しなければならない。なかなか一筋縄ではいかない問題である。

本稿では、GUNと堀川紀夫に焦点をあてて、展覧会準備で得られた知見をもとに、行為と情報の問題を考えたい。

1. GUNのメディア志向
–

GUNの1970年作品《雪のイメージを変えるイベント》は、もともとGUNが雪国・新潟で雪を使って何かしたいと考えていたところに、写真家・羽永光利がプロデューサー的役割を兼ねた協働者として関わって、GUNの構想が具体化し、実現にこぎつけた。本展の報道インタビューや関連プログラムでも（これまで同様に）、堀川紀夫と前山忠が率直に認めていたように、そもそも観客を求めて告知をしたわけでもなく、現場となった信濃川河川敷を見下ろす橋を通るバスに乗っていた乗客がちらりと見たかもしれない、というのが実情。最初から写真家を目撃者として実行されたプロジェクトである。[2] 第1回の実行には、羽永とその後輩の磯俊一が撮影、4日後の第2回目は羽永が撮影。この日は日曜日で、週実施の第1回に参加できなかった前山なども参加、また顔料を提供した海上雅臣（当時カラー・プランニング・センター重役）も東京から来て橋の上から見物し、あわせて10人程度の観客がいたのではないか、という。

今回新たに分かったのは、事前に予行演習があったことだ。漫画雑誌『少年サンデー』1971年3月21日号の珍奇な芸術特集で「地球がカンバスだ!!」の見出しで掲載されているのがその写真である。その時の描画は、市橋哲夫のアイディアで、幾何学抽象だったが、写真家二人とも満足できる写真がとれず、夕食に合流した堀川たちを交えて相談し、本番は「オートマティズム」でいくこと、堀川が褌姿でパフォーマンスすること、などを決めた。[3] こうして本番では自由に4色の顔料をスプレイペイントする、いわばジェス

チャー系抽象のカラーフィールドが現出した。

こうして行為し、撮影された写真が羽永を通じて『アサヒグラフ』に、磯を通じて『芸術生活』にカラー掲載され、当初の目的（マスメディアでのパブリシティ）は達成されたことになる。さらに、1972年に講談社から刊行された『現代の美術11：行為に賭ける』のブックカバーの裏表紙に採用されて、美術の文脈でもパブリシティを果たした。

なお、GUNの兄貴分であり、反芸術作家たちの行為を撮影してきた羽永は雪のイベントに多大な貢献をしたが、1980年代中ごろに堀川は羽永から雪のイベントのネガやポジを預かり、その後写真クレジットを明記しつつ、GUNの作品として図版に掲載したり、展覧会で写真やスライドで紹介するほかに、2009年には市橋哲夫、前山忠と共同してポートフォリオを制作している。GUNが〈目撃者〉としての羽永を尊重しながら、〈情報主体〉への意識を明確にした経過が垣間見える。現在は、2013年に結成された羽永光利プロジェクト委員会にネガとポジを返却しているが、画像は引き続きGUNの〈作品〉として展観している。本展でも、この形式を踏んで出品した。

2. 堀川紀夫──データカードという情報戦略
–

堀川紀夫の《石を送るメール・アート》は、アポロ計画に触発されて、月の石ならぬ地球の石を拾って郵送するという行為の作品である。作品のモノとして、郵送された石がいくつか残っている。行為の記録として「自分宛の郵送」をしたほかに、1969年7月のアポロ11号と連動した一番最初の郵送からデータカードも制作している。

データカードは 20×20 cm の大きさで、右下にTITLE、NAME、DATEを記す欄が印刷されている。これは、荒川修作が建築の青焼き設計図から発想した《ダイアグラム絵画》に倣ったもので、実際には瀧口修造が1968年に出版した『マルセル・デュシャン語録』に特別掲載されていた荒川作品を見て直接のヒントを得ている。

It should be remembered that the concept of the autonomy of a work as a self-sufficient entity is modern, itself requiring deconstruction. Furthermore, the museum as a modern apparatus that collects and displays "works" thus understood, thereby enforces the autonomy of art. The whole gamut of modernity in art will have to be reassessed in this regard but it goes beyond the scope of this essay. Here, I would like to refine my argument on act and information, based on the observations gained through my exhibition preparation as related to GUN and Horikawa Michio.

1. GUN's Media Orientation
—

GUN's 1970 work *Event to Change the Image of Snow* began with the collective's desire to do something with snow, the ubiquitous material of the snow country Niigata, their hometown. A catalyzing role was played by the photographer Hanaga Mitsutoshi, who joined their endeavor as a collaborator-producer, who in effect encouraged them to realize it. As two lead members Horikawa Michio and Maeyama Tadashi had frankly acknowledged (and did so again in the exhibition-related programs and interviews), the group did not actively seek an audience from their locale. No notice was given in advance; on the day of the event, it might have been glimpsed by a handful of passengers on buses passing the bridge that overlooked the site of their act, a vast dry riverbed of the Shinano River. From the beginning, they undertook the project to be witnessed by the photographer.[2] The first performance was photographed by Hanaga and his junior colleague Iso Toshikazu. The second performance was undertaken four days later on a Sunday, joined by Maeyama and others who had been absent on the first weekday undertaking. Hanaga alone photographed the performance. Unagami Masaomi, then an executive of Color Planning Center in Tokyo, who had contributed a massive amount of color pigments, came to see it from the best audience seat, that is, on the bridge. Horikawa and Maeyama recall altogether an audience of ten or so who watched the second act there.

A new discovery I made this time was that there was a dry run before the first performance. The photo-

graph was subsequently used in "Earth Is Our Canvas!" included in a special feature on extraordinary art works in the March 21, 1971 issue of the manga magazine *Shōnen Sunday*. For the rehearsal, they created a geometric abstraction proposed by the member Ichihashi Tetsuo, but the two photographers were utterly dissatisfied. Over the dinner that evening, they had a meeting, joined by Horikawa. They decided to use automatism on the following day, and have an additional event undertaken by Horikawa naked except for a loincloth.[3] Thus, for the first performance, the members freely sprayed four colors on the snow, creating a gestural abstraction of color fields.

The photographs were published in two magazines, *Asahi Graph* and *Geijutsu seikatsu* (Art life), thanks to the mediation of Hanaga and Iso respectively. The initial goal of gaining publicity in the mass media was thus achieved. They went on to be included in *Art of Action and Concept*, the eleventh volume of the *Art Now* series (published by Kōdansha in 1972). They were even featured on the back of the volume's dust jacket and a promotional flier, achieving exposure in the context of art history, as well.

Hanaga, who acted as a big brother to the younger GUN members, was known for photographing Anti-Art performances. His experiences made him a superb producer of GUN's snow event. Notably, in the mid-1980s, Horikawa asked Hanaga to entrust him with the negatives and positives of the snow-event photographs. Horikawa's intention was to use them as GUN's work in exhibitions and publications, with due credit given to the photographer. In 2009, together with Maeyama and Ichihashi, Horikawa published a limited-edition portfolio of photographs by Hanaga and Iso as GUN's work. Horikawa and his GUN colleagues clearly demonstrated their awareness of being the primary agency of information management for their event, while respecting the creative endeavor by the photographers-witnesses. In 2013, Horikawa returned the negatives and positives to the estate of the late photographer, but have since continued to display and publish the images as GUN's work. The exhibition at Japan Society followed this precedent.

念のため、メール・アートがパフォーマンス・アートなのか、という論点に触れておく。GUNの《雪のイメージを変えるイベント》に戻って考えるなら、それは広い大地をつかったランド・アートであり、雪をカンバスにした絵画であり、通常の描画をこえた行為だった点でパフォーマンス・アートでもある。Aか、Bか、というカテゴリーの二者択一は、ほぼ無意味ではないだろうか。

同様に「メール・ハプニング」[4]として構想された《石を送るメール・アート》は、郵送なる行為を接点としてメール・アートでありパフォーマンス・アートでもある。しかも、石を送られた側でも、一種の異化作用がおこり、字義通りのハプニング（意外な出来事）が生起する。

これらのデータカードを最初に見たのは、2001年にテートモダンで開催された「センチュリー・シティ」展のための調査に作家を訪れた時だった。何を尋ねたか今では思い出せないが、限りなく的外れな質問をした私に、「とりあえず、これを見てください」と渡されたのが、データカードをまとめたクリアフォルダーだった、と記憶する。ページを繰りながら「これは〈作品〉だ」との印象をもち、直感的に石と一緒に出品を考えていた。特に、アポロ11号にちなんだ第1回の《The Shinano River Plan: 11》のデータカードは、堀川が学校の新聞に寄稿した小文とともに、宛先人リストや現場写真などが貼りこまれて、小粒ながら包括的なプロジェクト概要となっていた。

本展でもほぼ同じ内容で、新旧の石とともに一連のデータカードを展観した。今回新発見だったのは、この第1回のデータカードが、雪の関連作品で展示しているデニス・オッペンハイムの1968年ランド・アート作品《境界線の分割》のパネルと構造的には変わらない、という事実である。つまり、行為に関する情報をパッケージ化している点は同じなのだ。

大きな違いはスケールだ。現代美術市場の機能しているニューヨークで活動していたオッペンハイムの大型パネル（60×40インチ＝154×101cm、90号Fに相当）は、準・絵画の美術館に収蔵されうる作品＝商品のスケールを確保している[5]。対して、市場経済の中にいない堀川ではスケールが小さく記録性にとどまっていることも確かだ。

しかしながら、小さいから劣っているとは限らない。オッペンハイムの場合には、雪関連もふくめてランド・アート作品を同工異曲でパネル化している。その戦略は定式化されて、それ自体には展開が無いように思われる。

一方で、堀川におけるデータカードの機動性は見逃せない。第1回郵送を延長させた8月の郵送では、石を受け取った赤塚行雄と南画廊の志水楠男から受領を知らせる郵便物が届いている。これを堀川はデータカードに貼りつけて、自らの作品に取り込んだ。

それだけではない。領収書を通じたコミュニケーションの連鎖に気付き、それを意図的に作り出すべく、1969年11月のアポロ12号にちなんだ郵送では、12個の石を石屋に半分に切らせ、それぞれの石について領収書を発行してもらい、それらを発送した郵便局でもそれぞれに領収書を発行してもらい、計12組24枚の領収書を貼りこんだデータカードを作成。東京などに出て、石を宛てた人たちに会う機会のあったときに、受領を確認しサイン（副署）してもらう、という手続きを考案し、東京画廊の山本孝や李禹煥など5人から副署を獲得した。データカードを作ることで、石の郵送をめぐる思考が進んでいったことがわかる。

3. 精神生理学研究所と堀川紀夫
–

上述の瀧口修造の『マルセル・デュシャン語録』は、デュシャンゆかりの作家たちによる版画セットを組みあわせた豪華版で、堀川は中学教師の薄給から無理をして購入した、と以前から聞いていた。が、今回初めて、データカードの起源を質問した[6]。

「数十枚の単位」で、厚めの紙（カードストック）に印刷したもので、当初は「色々な作品構想を描き、冊子のようにしよう」と考えたが、うまくいかなかったらしい。実際、1969年当時、様々な作品構想を記したノートが残されていて、こういうアイディアをアー

2. Horikawa Michio's
   Information Strategy: Data Cards
–

Horikawa's *Mail Art by Sending Stones* was inspired by the Apollo 11 mission. The series consists of acts of gathering earth stones—instead of the moon rocks picked up by astronauts—and mailing them. Several stones that he mailed are known to exist, which constitute the objecthood of the project. In addition, he made it a rule to send a stone to himself as a record and created data cards to collate related information, since the first mailing on July 21, 1969.

The artist had his data cards, measuring 20×20 centimeters, custom printed on cardstock, with a box at the lower right corner, in which to fill "title," "name," and "date." The data box was borrowed from Shūsaku Arakawa's so-called "diagram painting" series which was inspired by architectural blueprints that routinely include such data boxes. Horikawa saw an example of Arakawa's work in the deluxe edition of *Maruseru Dushan goroku/To and from Rrose Selavy: Selected Words of Marcel Duchamp*, translated and edited by the critic Takiguchi Shūzō.

Some may wonder whether mail art is performance art. These labels are often overlapping. Take, for example, GUN's *Event to Change the Image of Snow*. It is at once land art (working on a vast area of land directly), painting (literally they spray-painted on the snow as canvas), and finally performance art in that their act exceeded the conventional notion of "painting."

Likewise, Horikawa conceptualized his mail art as "Mail Happening," as noted in one of his earliest data cards.[4] It is at once mail art and performance art, mediated by the post office. Moreover, when a stone arrives to its designated recipient, a kind of dissimilation occurs due to this "unexpected event" which constitutes the dictionary definition of "happening."

I first saw his data cards during my research for *Century City*, the inaugural exhibition of Tate Modern in 2001. I cannot recall now what I asked him then, but it must have been fatally off the point. The artist told me, "Why don't you take a look at this," handing me a binder in which he had collated all these data cards. As

I paged through it, I was saying to myself, "This is not a 'document,' this is a 'work.'" On the spot, I knew I had to show them together with the extant stones. Especially memorable to me was the card bearing a short text the artist published in his school's student paper, small documentary photos, and the list of addressees. Tiny as it may be, it served as a succinct project summary.

In Japan Society's exhibition, I also presented a series of data cards along with the stones. A major discovery I made is the comparative display of this data card from *The Shinano River Plan: 11* and Dennis Oppenheim's *Boundary Split*, a panel of 1968, one year before Horikawa's mailing (unfortunately, not side by side but in two different rooms). Each of them serves as a project summary of an ephemeral performative work and the two share a cumulative collaged structure in presenting the project data. That is to say, they both packaged the information related to their acts as their "works."

One significant difference is scale. Active in New York, where the market for contemporary art was functional, Oppenheim created a large panel of 60 by 40 inches, which asserts a painting-like objecthood, marketplace viability, and museological presence.[5] In contrast, Horikawa, with no expectation of reward from the marketplace, was content with making a small card, the main function of which was indeed documentary.

It would be a mistake to judge the work by its size. Making a panel like *Boundary Split* was part of Oppenheim's performative works. There are a number of similar panels based on other land-art works he created. Of itself, the panel is relatively standard within his oeuvre, revealing little significant evolution.

For Horikawa, his data-cards became an effective site to reflect on his project. In the August 1969 mailing, executed as an extension of the first Apollo 11–inspired mailing, Horikawa received two notices of reception, one from the critic Akatsuka Yukio and the other from Shimizu Kusuo of Minami Gallery. He immediately incorporated them into his work by pasting them onto data cards.

This prompted him to see the potential for orchestrating a communication network based on receipts. For the mailing in conjunction with the Apollo 12 mis-

ティスト・ブックに仕立てようとしたのかと想像される[7]。こうして準備したカードが当初の目的には使えなかったものの、《石を送るメール・アート》で役立つことになる。

少し長くなるが、堀川メールの返信から引用してみよう。

その後、石を送ることを思いついて、その用紙を使いました。郵送で手紙や荷物は送ると、自分の手もとからなくなり相手に届くわけです。自分のところからなくなるもので自分のところに残せるもの。自分のところに残せる方法で、備忘のためにその控えを取っておくことがあります。石を送る場合、重さによって送料が変わります。その送付した相手、日付や重さや料金を記録しておく。郵便局でいただいたレシート。形状を写真で記録しておくこと。送付先から返礼としていただいたものなどを貼り付けて保管するため。一連の郵送行為を構成するその部分情報を自分の記録として作成したもので、当初は作品としての意識はありませんでした。

これを〈作品〉と思うようになったきっかけが、精神生理学研究所への参加だった、という点は着目に値する。これは当時東京造形大学の学生だった稲憲一郎と竹田潔が中心となって、ゼミのために期間限定でおこなった集団メール・アートで、1969年12月から1970年5月まで6回のメーリングが行われた。「規定された時空間において同時多発に行為あるいは無行為をもって参加する不可視的美術館」として、精神生理学研究所を定義し、「直接的なかかわりを拒否した個人の行為あるいは無行為の記録を 集合 離散させる」[8]ことを目指す。

参加者は、行為の後に〈報告〉を本部に郵送する。これは写真だったり、図表だったり、文章だったりするが、これを本部（稲と竹田）が複写して各回の参加者全員に郵送した。まずは、マルチプルとしてのモノが先行したわけだが、活動終了後の1970年8月に参加作品68点をA4のカードにオフセット印刷してポート

フォリオ形式にまとめた作品集を出版していた。つまりは、行為にまつわる情報をパッケージ化していた、と理解できる。

すなわち、日本の戦後美術史上、印刷版《精神生理学研究所》は意識的に情報をパッケージ化して、行為にモノとしての〈作品〉の形を与えた初期の例だった、ということになる。これまで何度となく見ていた精神生理学研究所だが、この位置付けも本展をつうじて得た知見だった。

先人もふくめて他人の作品から学びつつ自らの作品を作っていく堀川の方法論は〈インターポエティック〉という概念で理解できる。

いわゆる「複数のモダニズム」(multiple modernisms)の考え方を基礎にグローバルな視点を掲げつつ「世界美術史」を構築しようとすると、どうしても欧米中心史観の根幹にある中心が〈オリジナル〉で、周縁は〈影響〉を受けて〈模倣〉する、とみなす態度を再考しなくては先に進めない。インターポエティックは「相互詩学的関係」としてミン・ティアンポが『GUTAI：周縁からの挑戦』(三元社、2016年)で提唱した考え方だ。文学における〈オリジナリティ〉と〈影響〉を論じた文芸評論家のハロルド・ブルームから借用した概念で[9]、先人から学びつつ、それを土台に自らの創造性を発揮し積み上げていく芸術制作のあり方を意味する。

学習能力が高い作家だ、と言ってしまえばそれまでかもしれない。しかし、データカードによる一貫した記録を続け、その作業を通じて、データカードの意味するところを自ら理解していった道筋は、いまだ誰も解答を出していない方程式を解くのに似ていなくもない。近代に批判的に向き合い、現代の新しい表現をめざした堀川は[10]、安易な模倣に堕すことなく、よく学びよく作り、その実践の中で思考を続けた、と積極的に評価したい。

＊ ＊ ＊

総じて、さまざまな経緯はあるものの、〈荒野〉の行為者であるGUNと堀川紀夫は、行為にまつわる情

sion later in 1969, he had a stone-cutter halve twelve stones and issue twelve receipts for respective cutting. He further received twelve postage receipts from the post office upon mailing them. In total, he got twelve pairs of receipts. He pasted them on his data cards, one each on a card. On his subsequent excursions to Tokyo, he brought them with him. When the artist happened to meet with a recipient, he would strike up a conversation with him and ask him to countersign two cards bearing the related receipts. Horikawa successfully collected signatures from five recipients, including Yamamoto Takashi of Tokyo Gallery and the artist Lee Ufan. His data-card system thus enabled him to expand his communication strategy in mail art.

3. Horikawa Michio and
Psychophysiology Research Institute

–

The aforementioned *Selected Words of Marcel Duchamp* is the deluxe edition which came with a set of five prints by Duchamp himself and other artists. I have known that Horikawa acquired this special edition from his modest salary of a middle-school teacher. On the occasion of the Japan Society exhibition, I for the first time asked about the production of his data cards.[6]

He had "tens of them" printed on cardstock, a type of thicker paper, in order to "draw his ideas for new works on them and bind them." However, this plan did not work out. There is a notebook in which he made notes of such ideas from around 1969. He must have thought of transforming these "paper works" (like "paper architectures") into an artist's book.[7] Although these cards were not used for his initial plan, they turned out to be quite effective for his *Mail Art by Sending Stones*.

Let me quote his e-mail response:

Later, I thought of sending stones, and I used these cards. When you mail letters and packages, they will be delivered to recipients but you have nothing left in your hands. How to keep with me what will disappear from my place? One way was to make a memo by creating a *hikae* (record). When you send a stone, the postage varies depending on the weight. So, you

may make a note of an addressee, date, weight, and postage. You get a receipt at the post office. You take a photograph of the stone's form. Some recipients may acknowledge their receptions by mailing me something, which can be preserved on these cards. I made these cards in order to document a series of actions that constituted my mailing. In the beginning, I didn't think of it as a "work."

It is notable that Horikawa came to recognize them as his "work" as such when he participated in Psychophysiology Research Institute (Seishin Seirigaku Kenkyūjo; hereafter PRI). A mail-art collective, PRI was organized by Ina Ken'ichirō and Takeda Kiyoshi, then students at Tokyo Zōkei University, as a seminar project from December 1969 to May 1970. Altogether six mailings were undertaken. The organizers defined the project as "an invisible museum to which [participants] will each contribute through an act (*kōi*) or non-act undertaken simultaneously with others, where it can be positioned at a specified time-space." Their goal was to "accumulate and disperse the record of the acts or non-acts undertaken by individuals who refuse to have direct connections," as its invitation letter proclaims.[8]

Participants were required to send a "report" (*hōkoku*) to the headquarters (Ina and Takeda) after their acts. Reports could be diagrams, texts, or photographs, all of which the headquarters would reproduce and distribute among the participants of each mailing. The project thus began with multiples as its objects; upon the completion of the project, it was compiled into a portfolio of 68 works printed offset on A4 cards in August 1970. In other words, they packaged the information about their acts in the style of the artist's book.

In postwar Japanese art history, the published version of *Psychophysiology Research Institute* represents an early instance of endowing acts with objecthood and consciously packaging their information as a work. The exhibition gave me an occasion to reexamine the portfolio, which I had seen many times, and renew my understanding of its historical significance.

Horikawa's methodology of learning from predecessors and contemporaries in order to create his own

報主体として、自覚的に情報を流通させていた。行為（パフォーマンス・アート）は〈肉体〉の身振りや身体性などを作品の内容とみなすものの、現実には行為が終わった後に、〈第二の人生〉として写真記録によって理解することが多い。しかしながら、行為の〈第二の人生〉に必要なのは、実は写真だけでない、写真もふくめた情報の総体が作品の〈余生〉を担保する。行為が終わった後は、情報が作品である、との読みかえには異議があるかもしれない。しかしながら、情報を誰が保有し、流通させているか。このことを抜きには行為やパフォーマンス・アートは語れない。それを本展の企画と準備を通して痛感した。

【注】
1 富井玲子「平田実の《ACTION, the 1960s》──〈フォトアート〉の理論的考察」、平田実『ACTION, the 1960s』（展覧会図録）、Taka Ishii Gallery Photography/Film、2014 年。
2 篠原有司男の『前衛の道』を参照した学習効果も見逃せない。そのベースとなる『美術手帖』への連載を堀川は読んでいる。
3 堀川紀夫、筆者への電子メール、2019 年 3 月 25 日。
4 堀川紀夫「To Apollo 11」1969 年 7 月 21 日付データカード。
5 オッペンハイムが最初に行為の作品をパネル化したのか、を確認する必要が残っている。たとえば、堀川が見ていて、本展でも展観している『美術手帖』1969 年 7 月号の特集「新しい自然──エレメンタリズム〈アースワーク〉」では、オッペンハイムをふくめて写真は掲載されているが、情報をパネル化したものは図版掲載されていない。
6 堀川紀夫、筆者への電子メール、2019 年 3 月 22 日。
7 類似のアイディアで、堀川は東京ビエンナーレに出品した石の記録をエディションでアーティスト・ブックに仕立てて毎日新聞社で担当だった峯村敏明に郵送している。
8 精神生理学研究所、新潟研究所（堀川紀夫）にあてた参加依頼の手紙、1969 年 11 月 19 日付、堀川紀夫所蔵。
9 Harold Bloom, *The Anxiety of Influence* (Oxford: Oxford University Press, 1973).
10 堀川の作品構想を記したノートで、関根伸夫が 1969 年箱根彫刻の森美術館で開催された「第一回現代国際彫刻展」でコンクール賞を受賞した《空相》を分析している。「このエネルギーが現代である。これまでこのエネルギーがなくても石を石として考えることができた。現代をとらえて、近代を超克する」と記している。日付は石の郵送を思いついたのと同日の 1969 年 7 月 17 日。

初出：富井玲子「GUN における行為と情報──『荒野のラジカリズム』展補遺」『美術運動史』172 号（2019 年 4 月 20 日）1–7 頁。出版テキストでは最後に松澤宥とザ・プレイについても略述しているが、ここでは割愛した。

work can be understood as "interpoetic."

If we are to uphold a global perspective and build a world art history on the foundational concept of multiple modernisms, we cannot avoid revisiting Eurocentrism, whereby the center (Euro-America) was regarded the "originator" and the periphery, the "imitator" under the center's "influence." As a remedy to this ingrained view, the notion of "interpoetic" was first proposed by Ming Tiampo in her study *Gutai: Decentering Modernism* (University of Chicago Press, 2011). This is a b orrowing from the literary critic Harold Bloom, who examined originality and influence in literature.[9] In essence, artistic creation is a cumulative process consisting of what an artist learns from predecessors and what he or she develops from it through her/his creativity.

Indeed, Horikawa is a good student. But that's not all. Beginning with the system of data cards for documentation, he came to realize the potential of his system and eventually recognize them as "work," not just "document." The process is akin to solving an equation with no known solution. Critically looking at modernism and aspiring to create a new contemporary expression,[10] he did not follow a facile path of imitation. He studied well, made well, and thought well, as he put his ideas into practice.

* * *

Practitioners in the wilderness, GUN and Horikawa Michio became aware of their agency as the disseminator of information about their acts. An act, or performance art, can be gestural, bodily, and otherwise task-related. In reality, after a given act is completed, we routinely understand it through photographic records as its "second life." However, photography is not the only means for creating a second life. What warrants the second life as "work" is the entirety of information resulting from it. Some may object to my formulation that the information becomes a work after the completion of an act. Yet, we cannot understand performance art without considering who maintains and disseminates the information. This is what I learned through the exhibition at Japan Society.

[Notes]

1 Reiko Tomii, "Hirata Minoru's Action, the 1960s: A Theoretical Consideration as 'Photo Art,'" in *Hirata Minori: Action, the 1960s*, exh. cat. (Tokyo: Taka Ishii Gallery Photography/Film, 2014).

2 Horikawa was also familiar with and influenced by Shinohara Ushio's book *Avant-Garde Road*. He read it when the series was initially published in the magazine *Bijutsu techō*.

3 Horikawa Michio, e-mail to the author, March 25, 2019.

4 Horikawa, "To Apollo 11," handwritten data card, July 21, 1969.

5 We still need to ascertain when Oppenheim first turned the information into these panels. The July 1969 issue of *Bijutsu techō*, in which Horikawa saw many examples of land art in the special feature "New Nature: Elementalism, Earthworks," reproduces documentary photographs of Oppenheim's acts, not the panels.

6 Horikawa Michio, e-mail to the author, March 22, 2019.

7 With his stone mailing for *Tokyo Biennale 1970*, Horikawa created an editioned artist's book to document his mailing and sent a copy to Minemura Toshiaki of the Mainichi newspaper company who was in charge of the exhibition.

8 Psychophysiology Research Institute, initial request letter [to Niigata], November 19, 1969 (in the collection of Horikawa Michio).

9 Harold Bloom, *The Anxiety of Influence* (Oxford: Oxford University Press, 1973).

10 In his notebook, devoted to the inscription of ideas for new works, Horikawa analyzed Sekine Nobuo's *Phase of Nothingness*, which won an award at Hakone Open-Air Museum's *First Contemporary International Sculpture Exhibition* (1969), annotating, "This energy represents *gendai* 'contemporary.' [This work] transcends *kindai* (modern) by capturing *gendai*," on the page dated July 17, 1969, the very same day he thought of mailing stones.

(Translated from the Japanese original by the author)

Originally published as Reiko Tomii, "GUN ni okeru kōi to jōhō: 'Kōya no rajikarizumu' ten hoi" [GUN: Act and information: A reflection on the exhibition *Radicalism in the Wilderness*], *Bijutsu undōshi / Art Action History*, no. 172 (April 20, 2019): 1–7. Short discussions on Matsuzawa Yutaka and The Play included in the end of the original essay are omitted.

Text 3
Reiko Tomii

2000.12 某日《石》を初めてキュレーションした記念に思いがけず送っていただいた。ゲッティ研究所に寄贈する直前に撮影したが、黒いいびつな形態で座りが悪く、片手で持った図柄が一番決まっていた。ずっしりと重い感覚を今も覚えている（談・撮影：富井玲子）

= One day in December 2000, I unexpectedly receive a *Stone* that Horikawa sent me to commemorate my very first curation of his series. This photograph was subsequently made before its donation to the Getty Research Institute. The black *Stone* was irregularly shaped and difficult to "pose." The best shot was taken when I held it in my left hand while holding a camera on my right hand. I still remember the weighty presence I felt in my hand. (Reiko Tomii)

〈荒野〉と〈国際的同時性〉
── 《石を送るメール・アート》から考える世界美術史戦略
–

富井玲子

世界美術史への道

歴史は流動する。たとえ歴史の事象自体が変わらない場合でも、私たちがそれらの事象を見る眼が変わっていく。世界美術史は、歴史の流動性を体現する新しい世界観だ。

〈生きた〉言葉
–

世界美術史の定義は一定ではないが、戦後美術の場合、現在では広く共有されるようになった「複数のモダニズム」という脱中心化の地政学的歴史観を前提として語られることが多い。少なくとも私は、そのような企図だと認識している。この中で、戦後日本の作品や作家をどう具体的に位置付けていくか。この問題意識を主要なモチベーションとして執筆したのが、コンセプチュアリズムを先駆した松澤宥、野心的なハプニングを風景の中に繰り広げたザ・プレイ、雪上絵画から政治意識の高い表現へと展開したGUN、の3作家・集団を中心に論じた拙著『荒野のラジカリズム ── 国際的同時性と日本の1960年代美術』(MIT出版、2016年)だった。

この間、私は一貫して、可能な限り研究対象となる時代 ── 1960年代 ── を生きた人々から学ぶことを方法論の基本の一つにしてきた。1957年に生まれた私にとって、60年代は未熟な子供の目で見た世界でしかない。全くの未経験ではなかったが〈学習〉は不可欠であり、当事者の言葉を聞くことは時代を理解するために何より効果的な方法だった。オーラルヒストリー（聴き取り調査）などによる〈回顧〉の言葉もあれば、雑誌などに出版されたもの、あるいは人知れずノート類に記されていた〈当時〉の言葉もあった。もちろん、これは時代を問わず歴史研究の基本だが、本人に聞いてみなければわからない作家の〈思考〉や〈判断〉を〈生きた〉言葉として聞けたのは、近過去の美術表現を研究する醍醐味でもあった。

拙著の表題に選び、本論のタイトルにも掲げた〈荒野〉と〈国際的同時性〉は、まさにそうして私が学ん だ〈生きた〉言葉に他ならない。

作家の〈判断〉
–

ところで〈生きた〉言葉は、今を生きる歴史家の現実にも存在する。歴史を物語るとは、畢竟現在に立ち位置を持ちつつ、過去を読み且つ語ることだからだ。

2005年にさかのぼるが、戦後日本美術史研究グループのポンジャ現懇の主宰で、イエール大学と共同でポンジャ現懇第1回シンポジウムを開催した。その時ディスカッサントとして招聘したモダニズムの専門家、同大学（当時）のデービッド・ジョスリット教授が、日本の60年代美術の革新性を高く評価する感想（と驚き）を語ったので、パネルの後で個人的に「では今後、先生の60年代美術講義に日本を取り入れますか」と質問した。私は具体や反芸術や非芸術の作品群の歴史的意義を確信していたから、彼の答えが「否」だったので驚いた。思わず「何故ですか」と問い返したら、教授は「作家の判断がわからないから」と答えた。

作家の〈判断〉(an artist's judgement) ── これは深い言葉だ。作品を構想し制作するにあたって、作家が何を意図し、何をどう斟酌して、そのモチーフを選んだのか、あるいは絵筆を擱くことを決めたのか。たとえば、セザンヌの空白の背後にはどんな作家の判断が横たわっているのだろうか。たとえば、ポロックが制作途中の大カンバスを見つめながら、その周囲を歩きながら、どんな判断をしているのだろうか。

何より1960年代は現代美術の転換期で、近代的な自律した絵画彫刻をめぐる作品思考からの離脱が大々的に世界各地で同時多発的に起こっていた。具体、反芸術、非芸術という日本の60年代美術の動向も〈国際的同時性〉を形成する潮流の一つだった。だが、近代思考からの離脱にいたる道筋はいかにつくられたのか。いかなる意図と判断と決断をもって個々の作家たちは新しい表現を作っていったのか。それらが理解できなければ、60年代美術を真に語ることはできないだろう。それは造形思考だけの問題ではない。表

"Wilderness" and "International Contemporaneity": A Strategy for World Art History, as Seen from *Mail Art by Sending Stones*

—

Reiko Tomii

A Road to World Art History

History is prone to changes. Even when historical events themselves do not change, our eye that sees them changes. Embodying this very nature of history, world art history presents a new worldview.

"Living" Words
—

The definition of world art history is still fluid. However, in postwar art, the now widely shared notion of "multiple modernisms" informed a decentered geohistorical perspective of the discipline. Or, at least, that is how I understand it. How to concretely position postwar Japanese artists and their works in this framework? This question was the primary motivation of mine to author *Radicalism in the Wilderness: International Contemporaneity and 1960s Art in Japan* (MIT Press, 2016) that centers on three protagonists, Matsuzawa Yutaka, a conceptualist pioneer, The Play, a collective that undertook ambitious Happenings in landscapes, and GUN, a collective known for their snow painting and politically oriented mail art.

One of my research methodologies is to learn, as much as possible, directly from those who lived the 1960s, the period of my study. Born in 1957, I experienced the 1960s merely as a young child. It may be better than no experience at all, but learning is more than necessary. To learn from the words of those who experienced the time is an effective avenue of exploration. My study is retrospective in nature: some words derive from oral histories (interviews); some from the very moments, printed in magazines and other publications; yet others were inscribed in notebooks and such, unknown but to the writers themselves. Studying these words is a basic step for a historian of any era. In the case of art from the recent past, it is thrilling to gain direct access to the artist's thinking and judgement as "living words" in person.

Two terms, "wilderness" and "international contemporaneity" were such living words I found and adopted for my book and again in the title of this essay.

The Artist's "Judgement"
—

The importance of living words is not limited to artists, but concerns art historians, too. To narrate a history is to stand in the present and read the past and articulate a story about it.

In 2005, I had a crucial experience of hearing an art historian's living words. That year, as co-director of PoNJA-GenKon, a listserv group for postwar Japanese art history, I co-organized *The First PoNJA-GenKon Symposium* with Yale University. We invited David Joselit, a modernist and then professor of art history at Yale, as a discussant to my panel on 1960s art in Japan. As part of his commentary, he expressed his high appraisal of (and surprise at) the innovative nature of the works presented, including those of Gutai, conceptualism, and Mono-ha. After the proceedings, I personally asked him, "Will you then incorporate 1960s Japan in your classes?" To my surprise, his answer was no. I immediately asked why, and his explanation was, in essence, "I don't understand their judgements as artists."

An artist's judgement. This is a profound word. When the artist conceptualizes and makes a work, what does s/he intend or take into consideration in selecting a particular theme or deciding to put a brush down? For example, what judgement did Cézanne make when he left some part of his painting blank? What judgement did Pollock make as he walked around a huge canvas and observed its interim state?

We have to remember that the 1960s was a transformative decade, when the modern notion of the autonomy of art was challenged, as artists questioned the conventions of painting and sculpture in many parts of the world contemporaneously. Gutai, Anti-Art (*Han-geijutsu*), and Non-Art (*Hi-geijutsu*), which arose in the expanded 1960s, were among these new developments that contributed to the state of "international contemporaneity" (*kokusaiteki dōjisei*). How did individual artists formulate their paths to depart from the modern? What kind of thinking and judgement did they make to create new expressions? If we cannot give answers to these questions, we will not fully understand 1960s art. The issue is not limited to morphology.

現は完全に表現のみで自律しては存在しえないから、表現をとりまく文脈＝ローカル事情の問題でもある。

とすれば、欧米モダニズムを専門とする研究者の躊躇を無視してはならない。その躊躇を払拭、とまではいかなくとも少なくとも軽減できなければ、日本の戦後美術は世界美術史に根付かないだろうから——。

ただし、作家の判断は、必ずしもリアル・タイムで捕獲できるとは限らない。誤解を恐れずに譬えるなら、タイムマシンに乗って、その場その時の考えを作家に直撃インタビューしたとして、必ずしも作家が自分の判断を明確に言葉にしてくれるとは限らない。むしろアートは言語意識や論理的判断を超えた領域で思考が動くことも多い。作家本人が後から気づくことも稀ではない。作品を時間の流れの中でとらえ、個人の占める空間や社会の枠組の中で、さらにはより大きな時代の文脈の中で多角的に見ていくことにより、その作家の判断を探っていく。これは、作家のエージェンシー（翻訳が難しいが「主体性」が一応の意味を伝えてくれるが、一歩踏み込んで「能動的判断をする行動主体」としてもよいだろう）を基本にして、個々の作家、あるいは個々の作品を出発点としてグローバルに世界を考える〈ボトムアップ〉の視点でもある。しいて和訳するなら「足元から考える」あるいは「下から目線」となる。

〈ボトムアップ〉の視点
–

〈ボトムアップ〉の視点は、作家のエージェンシーを積極的に読み込んでいく視点である。作家がその時代を生きて経験したこと、経験から思考し行為したこと、それを学び、読み込んでいく。そんなポジティブな視点である。

ところで、いつも疑問に思うことがある。日本の作家たちは日本を「悪い場所」（椹木野衣）だと悲観し、諦念して生きていたのだろうか。ここで言われている「悪い場所」とは、「美術」が存在しなくて西洋から移入した地域と同義だから、畢竟「近代（美術）後進国」を意味する。

「悪い場所」論への批判はいくつもあるだろうが、大きな問題は、何が〈近代〉なのか、という点であり、暗黙に明治以来の近代化＝西洋化の等式で考えている、という点ではないだろうか。

現時点から逆照射するなら、近代とは、今日のグローバルな世界における「時空の共有化」の端緒だったのではないか、と私は考えている。その中で科学技術の優位性を背景に、西欧諸国が覇権主義で軍事力・経済力・植民地化（帝国主義）を行使して近代を〈先導〉した。回顧すれば西洋近代の人文科学の進展は非西洋（中近東やアジアなど）で蓄積されてきていた〈知〉に根差した展開も少なくなかったが、その事実や前史は忘却・隠蔽されて、西洋先導の強者の論理として近代の言説が立ち上がる。美術史もこの中にある。

印象派から始まる革新と実験の西洋美術の歴史が、実に豊饒な人間の創造性の追求だったことを認めるのはやぶさかではない。だが、西欧を「モダニズム先進国」とする歴史言説をいったん括弧入れする必要があるだろう。

では、その上で近代の歴史をどう語っていくのか、専門家の間でも意見は分かれる。かりに「時空共有」のプロセスとしての近代を考えるとするならば、非西洋とは、すなわち西洋の覇権行使の対象となる地域の謂いであり、死活問題として時空の共有化を受け入れる必要に迫られた。日本の黒船来航のエピソードは一つの例だろう。日本の社会・文化状況が、その時点で近代的進展を兆していたにも関わらず、（強制的）共有化の始まった時空の中で生きていくために西洋化としての近代化が始まる。江戸の近代がいかに明治の近代に接続していくのかは、分野々々で異なっている。が、全体として、日本に〈遅延〉の意識が生じる。「悪い場所」論が根本的な過誤だとは言えないのも、この理由による。

だが、非西洋の国々は多かれ少なかれ日本と同じ状況にあったわけで、日本が悪い場所ならば、世界中はとんど悪い場所だらけだったにちがいない。しかも、植民地化や政治弾圧、集団虐殺、強制収容などを経験した地域や集団もある。帝国願望を実現しつつあっ

The matter of expression does not exist in a complete vacuum; it is imbedded in the surrounding contexts, that is, local circumstances.

That is why I felt that we must not ignore the hesitation of Western modernists in looking at 1960s art in Japan. If we cannot totally eliminate their hesitation, we should at least assuage it; otherwise, postwar Japan will not be able to secure a stable place in world art history.

It should be noted that an artist's judgement cannot always be captured in real time. Were we to travel back to the very moment of the artist's act and ask him or her what is the thinking behind it, he or she might not be able to articulate it on the spot. Art necessarily involves thinking beyond verbal consciousness and logical decisions. The very artist may benefit from hindsight. An art historian's task (among many) is to understand the artist's judgement by placing the work in a flow of time while considering it in a number of aspects within the surrounding contexts, social and otherwise, and a larger framework within an era. The respect for the artist's agency is fundamental in a bottom-up methodology that begins with individual artists and their works to give their global relevance.

A Bottom-Up Perspective
–

The artist's agency is vital to a bottom-up perspective, which involves learning and reading about what the artist experienced in living in that era and as a result thought and acted from experiences.

In this regard, I have long had one nagging question: Were Japanese artists really so pessimistic, as the critic Sawaragi Noi formulated Japan to be a "bad place" in his notorious 1998 volume, *Nihon/Gendai/Bijutsu* (Japan/contemporary/art)? Herein, a "bad place" refers to a country that lacked the modern concept of "art" (*bijutsu*) and imported it from the West. In essence, it means a "latecomer to modernism."

Sawaragi's "bad place" discourse can be critiqued in a number of ways, but the fundamental issue is the definition of modernity, for the critic internalized the view of equating modernization and Westernization

that has been long held, indeed since the mid-19th century.

From the vantagepoint of today's globalization, I would like to propose that modernity was the process of sharing time-space, wherein the European nation-states "led" modernization by exercising their hegemonic powers, backed by their overwhelming military, economic, and colonizing (imperialist) forces. In retrospect, the West's modern achievements in humanities and sciences were not always pure Western inventions. Many were rooted in and informed by knowledge accumulated in non-Western areas (such as the Middle East and Asia) as much as in the West. Yet this fact was either suppressed or forgotten, and the discourse of modernity was formulated as a kind of winner's logic by the West. Art history is part of this hegemonic development.

The history of Western art built on experiments and innovations beginning with Impressionism certainly constitutes a splendid exploration of human creativity. Still, we need to bracket this historical discourse which equates the West with the "advanced countries of modernism."

How, then, to narrate a history of modernism? Opinions diverge among scholars and specialists. If we define modernity as the process of sharing time-space, the non-West was situated on the receiving end of the West's hegemonic powers, which forced the non-West to join the process of time-space sharing, often as a matter of life and death. Japan's opening following the visit of Commodore Perry in 1853 is one such dramatic episode. Although Japan by then developed certain distinct features of modernism, Westernization under the name of modernization began in order to survive in the time-space sharing process. The degree of incorporation of Edo modernity into Meiji modernity varied from discipline to discipline. Overall, however, the consciousness of "belatedness" emerged. In this sense, Sawaragi's view contains a kernel of truth.

Yet, we must remember that Japan was in a predicament similar to many non-Western countries. If Japan was a bad place, almost every other place was also a bad place. Furthermore, many other regions and peo-

た日本の「悪い場所度」はいかほどのものだったのか。

また、一般に、西洋、あるいは欧米と一括りにしているが、20世紀の半ばまでアメリカ美術もまた遅延意識に苦しみ、長くヨーロッパ・モダニズムの色あせた影とみなされていたからこそ、抽象表現主義による「アメリカ絵画の勝利」(アーヴィング・サンドラー)があれほどまでに誇らしかったに違いない。

たとえ(今から見れば)悪い場所だったとしても、西洋から近代の諸制度を移入し学習しながら、その土地々々の状況と論理(ロジック)に根差したモダニズムを形成していった、あるいは形成しようとした作家たちや文化に携わった人々は、その困難な企図に立ち向かい果敢に闘ってきたのではないだろうか。日本に限らず、その闘争と格闘(struggles)の総和としてそれぞれの地域のモダニズム(美術や文化)があり、それぞれの地域の近代がある。そう考えれば、本質主義的に日本らしいもの、日本に固有の表象のみが「日本的」を作るのではない。むしろ、近代において最もビビッドに「日本的」を規定するのは、そうした闘争と格闘の形なのではないだろうか。

その何よりの例が、後に触れるように、DIY精神に満ちた日本の美術団体だと私は考えている。むしろ、私の提唱する〈ボトムアップ〉の視点もまた、ボトムアップでモダニズムを構築してきた作家たちの生きた軌跡から学んだ視点だったと言うほうが正確だろう。

世界美術史において〈ボトムアップ〉の視点が重要なのは、複数のモダニズムの歴史を語るために〈遅延〉を見据えて、それを肯定的価値に転換させる可能性があるからだ。

世界の各地で「時空共有としての近代」への参画によりモダニズムの時間が流れ始める。多くの場合、遅延を伴いながらの出発だが、それぞれの時間の流れは均一ではなく、しかも遅延が恒久的に遅延にとどまるとは限らない。遅延の時間差が一挙に縮まったのが第二次世界大戦後のジェスチャー系抽象の登場であり、〈国際的同時性〉時代の幕が上がる。しかしながら、時空の共有は表現の画一性を意味しない。同時性が現出してもなお表出する多様性がモダニズムの真

髄でもある。たとえ、西洋近代を一種のベンチマークとして保留付きで歴史語りの便法として採用するとしても、多様性自体はトップダウンの西洋の(強者の)論理では説明できない。だからこそ、ボトムアップでローカルの視点を言説化していく意義がある。

実践的には、たとえば堀川紀夫の《石を送るメール・アート》を、欧米の戦後美術史の時系列に挿入あるいは追加しただけでは「歴史化」としては不十分だ。作家の〈判断〉を理解しうる形で根付かせなければ、一過性の興味に終わってしまいかねない。作家のエージェンシーとそれを取り巻く闘争の背景と状況をボトムアップで語りつつ、大枠の世界美術史へとつなげていくことが必要だ。

ボトムアップの視点が、ローカルの有効性と必然性を担保する。さらに、《石を送るメール・アート》論に焦点を当てるなら、ローカルの視点は〈荒野〉に繋留され、グローバルな視点は〈国際的同時性〉から立ち上がる。

世界美術史における《石を送るメール・アート》

ローカル：〈荒野〉の精神
—

〈荒野＝Wilderness〉は喚起力の豊饒な言葉だ。

直接の出典は、松澤宥の1964年の名作《荒野のアンデパンダン'64展》だった。美術雑誌の広告という「自律したモノ」としての作品に真っ向から対立した非物質的な表現を〈作品〉と宣言するのが、世界美術史へいたる私の作業の第一歩となった。同作品を展観した「グローバル・コンセプチュアリズム」展は、それまで広く流通していたコスースなどの作品を典型とする欧米中心で言語中心のコンセプチュアル・アート(＝概念芸術)の定義を根本から再検討しようとしており、世界美術史を予告する企図の一つとして評価されている。その試みの中で、松澤の革新性(ラジカリズム)と同時代性は、日本セクションの要だった。

この作品の〈荒野〉は、作家の自宅から遠くない八島湿原を指している。夏は全国から人が訪れて観光

128

ples suffered such brutalities as colonization, political oppression, genocide, and forced incarcerations. In this context, one may well stop to reflect on the "bad place" quotient of Japan that harbored an imperialist dream and acted on it.

At the same time, although we frequently talk about Euro-America as a single entity, the U.S. had long suffered from belatedness, with its modern art slighted as a pale reflection of European modernism. All the more so, the "triumph of American painting" (Irving Sandler) with Abstract Expressionism was sweet and uplifting.

Even if Japan was (in retrospect) a bad place, artists and other cultural practitioners struggled earnestly with the difficult project of formulating a locally rooted modernism while learning and introducing the modern institutions from the West. Not just in Japan, but in other "bad places," the sum total of such struggles characterizes a local modernism in art and culture and defines that locale. If so, then, these struggles more vividly make Japan Japanese in modern times, more so than what is Japanese in the essentialist sense.

Among such "Japanese" struggles is the prewar collectivism of *bijutsu dantai*, as will soon be touched upon. My bottom-up perspective, too, is learned from their lived experiences and informed by the bottom-up endeavors of Japanese artists to devise a local modernism.

The bottom-up perspective is important in world art history because it will help us reassess the notion of "belatedness" and incorporate potentially positive frameworks into a new narrative.

When various locales joined the time-space sharing process, a time of modernism began to flow at each of them. Time at each locale flowed at its own speed, often marked by temporary delays. In fact, after World War II, these gaps closed up with the rise of gestural abstraction worldwide, heralding an era of international contemporaneity. It should be noted that the sharing of time-space does not mean the homogeneity of expressions. Diversity despite contemporaneity is the most essential part of modernism. Even if we adopt Western modernism as a kind of benchmark for the

sake of narration, diverse expressions thus materialized cannot be explained by the top-down Western logic. That is why it is imperative to articulate the local perspectives in a bottom-up manner.

In creating a new narrative, it is insufficient to simply add or insert, say, Horikawa's *Mail Art by Sending Stones* to the existing chronology of (Euro-American) postwar art history. If the artist's judgement is not fully understood, it won't take root, although it may attract a fleeting or superfluous attention. A bottom-up narration of the artist's agency and what surrounded it then has to be linked to the larger story of world art history.

The bottom-up perspective warrants the efficacy and necessity of the local. In the case of *Mail Art by Sending Stones*, the artist's local struggle is tied to the "wilderness," while the global relevance is underscored by its "international contemporaneity."

Mail Art by Sending Stones in World Art History

Local: From the Spirit of "Wilderness"
–

"Wilderness" is a provocative word. I borrowed it from Matsuzawa Yutaka's 1964 masterpiece *Independent '64 in the Wilderness*. My first step in world art history was to declare this ad in an art magazine as a work (*sakuhin*), going against the convention that a *sakuhin* is an autonomous object. I presented it in *Global Conceptualism*, an exhibition that fundamentally reexamined the established Eurocentric definition of Conceptual Art (*Gainen geijutsu*) that prioritized language-based practices as exemplified by Kosuth. The exhibition was a prescient attempt at what would become world art history, in which I felt Matsuzawa's radicalism and contemporaneity was key to articulating the significance of the Japanese section.

The wilderness in Matsuzawa's work refers to Yashima Highland near his home in central Japan. During the summer, many tourists visit the highland designated as one of the nation's "natural monuments," but in December, it turns into a desolate landscape with no people around. It is a site fitting for the name of "wilderness." At the same time, the wilderness meant

地としてにぎわうが、12月の展覧会中は天然記念物に指定された高原も茫漠として無人の風景が広がる。まさに〈荒野〉という喚起力の強い言葉を体現する〈場〉でもある。さらに、東京＝中心に対する、周縁としての地方が、読売アンデパンダン展中止後に繰り広げた自主アンデパンダン運動への賛同を表明して存在感を発揮する。

『荒野のラジカリズム』の中で、彼方＝地方としての〈荒野〉に一番当てはまるのはGUNだろう。松澤が生涯の活動の地と定めた生地、下諏訪は甲州街道の終点で中山道六十九次のうち江戸からは29番目だから、交通の要衝で中心と繋がっていたし、諏訪大社を擁して独自の文化圏を形成していた。ザ・プレイの本拠地である関西は大阪、奈良、京都と古代から中世にかけて日本の中心だった。対して、GUNが本拠とした新潟県は東京から日本アルプスを貫通するトンネルを抜けてたどり着く『雪国』（川端康成）で、東京＝中心からの遠さは想像にあまりある。最初に東京から堀川を訪問した時、新潟県人・田中角栄の悲願であった上越新幹線を使っても、堀川の住む上越市（旧・高田市）までのローカル線は長かった。あの時の遠距離の感覚は今でも覚えている（現在は北陸新幹線が堀川の住む上越に止まるので、東京からの所要時間は格段に短縮された）。

この空間的距離、さらにはそこから派生する社会的・文化的距離が〈荒野〉の一つの意味ではあるが、もう一つ、東アジアには、在野という〈野〉がある。権力＝制度に対比する〈野〉は、中国では「下野＝野に下る」、日本では「在野＝野に在る」の熟語で知られている。古代中国の歴史物語を読んでいてワクワクするのは、『三国志』で活躍する諸葛孔明のように、野にある逸材を権力が召喚するエピソードが珍しくないことだ。野は必ずしも中央と敵対しない。むしろ野は制度に収まりきらない才能の宝庫であり、緊急時のリザーブですらある。

一方、日本の近代美術では、〈在野〉はコレクティヴィズム、すなわち美術団体を考えるためのキーワードでもある。いうまでもなく、国家の主催した官展への対抗として二科会や日本美術院が在野団体として結成されたわけだが、この経緯を〈表現〉における意見の不一致を乗り越えるために、新たな舞台（プラットフォーム）をオルタナティブに自前で設立して、作品を発表していくと読み解くなら、Do It Yourself（DIY）精神が日本の在野の真骨頂でもあったともいえる。こうしたポジティブな評価は、作家の活動を、（戦前には）主にアトリエで作業される〈表現〉と、表現を社会に提示する展覧会活動などを〈オペレーション〉に分解し、作家の社会的エージェンシーを前面化してみるとよりはっきりと見えてくる。

この理論的読解を進めると、ポスト読売の自主アンデパンダン展運動は、まさに団体展とは対極にある発想ながら、地方の作家たちがやはりDIYの精神を発揮して、荒野＝地方、すなわち権力の外側に自前の舞台を作り出したと理解できる。つまり、目標は異なるもののDIYが日本のモダニズムの通奏低音として聞こえてくる。

戦後のコレクティヴィズムは、より流動的な〈集団〉が戦前以上にはるかに大きな役割を果たす。美術団体の発展形態として50年代半ばに発足した具体を筆頭に、60年代にはハイレッド・センターやゼロ次元など小集団が林立し、60年代後半以降『荒野のラジカリズム』の主役であるザ・プレイやGUN、そして松澤宥のニルヴァーナ派に続いていき、それぞれ集団としてのオペレーションに新基軸を開いている。

この中で、GUNは地理的なハンデのみならず年齢の若さもあいまって、野にあることの困難が一番大きかっただろう。集団としてのGUNは、東京と新潟でグループ展の活動を1年間行い、1969年以降は資金枯渇とともに、展覧会以外の活動を地元で探りはじめた。1970年に地元新潟で行った《雪のイメージをかえるイベント》は全国メディアで成功したものの、グループとしての活動よりも、GUNの旗印をかかげての個人制作が主となっていく。

そもそも展覧会組織としての集団は、展覧会が途絶えると空中分解しがちだ。GUNも1969年の時点で破綻していても不思議ではなかった。だが、結成から1

regionalism on the margins within Japan, as opposed to the center Tokyo. Thus, the exhibition embodied Matsuzawa's sympathy for the movement of artist-organized independent exhibitions that had emerged after the suspension of the Yomiuri Independent Exhibition in January 1964.

In my book *Radicalism in the Wilderness*, GUN is the farthest from the center Tokyo, which made them the utmost wilderness practitioners among three. Matsuzawa's hometown, Shimo Suwa, which early on he decided to turn into the base of his operations used to be the endpoint of the Kōshū Highway and the 29th station from Edo of all the 69 stations of Nakasendō leading to Kyoto. In this regard, Shimo Suwa was a transportation hub, with a distinct culture sphere centering around the Suwa Shrine. Likewise, The Play was based in Kansai, where ancient capitals were located in Osaka, Nara, and Kyoto, constituting the old center of Japan. In contrast, Niigata, GUN's home, was a Snow Country, reachable only via a long tunnel bored through the Japan Alps, as the novelist Kawabata Yasunari described in his novel. The distance from the center Tokyo is beyond our imagination. I still remember how long it felt to visit Horikawa from Tokyo for the first time. Back then, I had to combine the Jōetsu bullet train, the dream project of the Niigata-born Prime Minister Tanaka Kakuei, and a local line to the city of Jōetsu (formerly Takada), where he resided. (The distance has been reduced exponentially by the Hokuriu bullet train that stops at Horikawa's hometown Jōetsu.)

This spatial distance, together with the social and cultural distance induced by it, constitutes the wilderness. Additionally, in the history of East Asia, there was the wilderness (荒野) called *ya* (野), which existed in opposition to the political powers and other institutions. In China, politicians would "descend to the wilderness" (*xiaye*, 下野) when they lost their positions in the court and the government. In modern Japan, it gained a positive connotation as in "being in the wilderness" (*zaiya*, 在野), which means not participating in institutional systems. In the world of Chinese fiction, it is thrilling to read how gifted strategists in the

wilderness are summoned to help kings, like Zhuge Liang in *Records of the Three Kingdoms*. The wilderness is not necessarily antagonistic to powers that be, but is a reservoir of talents outside the institutions that can be tapped in times of emergency.

In modern Japanese art, the concept of *zaiya* is central to the prewar collectivism of *bijutsu dantai* (art organizations). *Zaiya* organizations, such as Nika (Second Section) Society and Japan Art Institute (Nihon Bijutsu-in), arose in opposition to the state-hosted salon. The two groups, and many others that would follow them, embody the DIY (do it yourself) spirit of the wilderness in Japan, which becomes evident when we foreground the artist's social agency. Which is to say, when we divide the artist's labor into "expression" (mainly produced within the studio in prewar contexts) and "operation" (mainly conducted outside the studio in the form of exhibitions), we can understand prewar collectivism as a strategy for artists to form an alternative base of "operation" in order to put forth their own "expression."

Within this conceptual framework, the post-Yomiuri movement of artist-organized independent exhibitions was informed by the same wilderness spirit of DIY, except for one major difference. Unlike prewar *dantai* collectives, many of which would become an integral part of the art establishment, post-Yomiuri artists sought to create a platform of operation *outside* the center outside Tokyo.

Postwar collectivism shifted from the prewar mode of *dantai* to the more flexible mode of smaller *shūdan* (collective). Beginning with Gutai, which is a hybrid of *dantai* and *shūdan*, founded in the 1950s, small *shūdan* proliferated in the 1960s, including Hi Red Center and Zero Jigen (Zero Dimension). From the late 1960s onward, The Play, GUN, and Matsuzawa's Nirvana School—three protagonists of *Radicalism in the Wilderness*—emerged to open new horizons in collective operation.

Among the three, due to their geography and youth, GUN's difficulty of being in the wilderness was most acute. As a collective, GUN undertook a series of group exhibitions in Tokyo and Niigata in their

年間旺盛にグループ展を連鎖させたおかげで新潟の前衛集団として一定の知名度が生まれていた。その利を活かして「GUNの堀川紀夫」あるいは「GUNの前山忠」を名刺代わりに活動を続けることで、まずは自前の活動母体（プラットフォーム）を確保したわけだ。集団としては変則的な活動形式だが、作家活動の選択肢が限られている地方の状況に対処した若い作家たちの苦肉の策だったに違いない。

ただし、オペレーション母体の確保はよいとして、作家の勝負は言うまでもなく表現にある。その模索の中から表現を展覧会制度の外に持ち出して堀川紀夫の《石を送るメール・アート》は生まれた。

展覧会は表現を社会に提示・伝達する〈オペレーション〉の典型的形式だが、60年代日本では、ハイレッド・センターの路上アクションに代表されるように展覧会制度の外側での表現の提示が起こり、〈表現〉（＝行為・情報）と〈オペレーション〉（＝社会への情報伝達）の場が一体化する動向が出てきた。ザ・プレイのハプニングでは、両者の一体化がさらに進み、事後の情報伝達を意識的に組織するとともに、コレクティヴのコンセプト自体をメンバー以外の協力者に拡張して社会に関与する次元も生み出した。

メール・アートもまた〈表現〉を展覧会の外に持ち出す。そして堀川の場合には、石が〈表現〉であると同時に石を送る行為が〈表現〉であり、かつ〈オペレーション〉でもあるという一体化が起こる。さらに、堀川は郵送行為の第二の人生となる「記録カード」も作品化して、情報のネットワークを積極的に作品として重層化した点が特筆に値する。

このように、コレクティヴィズムで導入した〈表現〉と〈オペレーション〉の考え方は、コンセプチュアリズムでも有効だ。作品を〈何を表現するのか＝情報〉と〈オペレーションとしてどう伝達するのか＝情報化〉に分解するなら、〈オペレーション〉を展覧会から郵送、直接提示、情報化まで幅のある〈スペクトラム〉に分析できるだろう。堀川の《石を送るメール・アート》は、物質の郵送や展示による直接提示から、送った石のみならず郵送という行為そのものを情報化し

ていて、幅広いオペレーションのスペクトラムを包括した表現になっている。

グローバル：〈国際的同時性〉と比較
—

さて、〈荒野〉において《石を送るメール・アート》を歴史化するということは、日本というローカルな文脈での話である。では、視点を世界に広げたグローバルな歴史化はどんな形をとるだろうか？

ここで、日本のみならず数々の非西洋と西洋のローカル・ヒストリーを包括するのが、1960年代にグローバルに前景化した〈国際的同時性〉という大きな枠組みである。出典は宮川淳と針生一郎の批評だ。〈遅延〉を意識していたからこそ、1960年代の日本では批評言説としての〈国際的同時性〉が立ち上がった。それを新たなナラティブとして言語化する方法論が比較美術史であり、私の場合には専門である1960年代日本をパラダイム・サイト（paradigm site）——つまりこれまでの美術史で常識とされてきた認識や思想、価値観などを抜本的に変革していくために「範例となるような場」として使いながら分析することになる。

一つの戦略は、〈似て非なる＝similar yet dissimilar〉作品を〈響きあい＝resonance〉に探り、実際の〈繋がり＝connection〉がなくとも、比較して新たなナラティブの接線を見出し輻輳していくことだ。たとえば、分かりやすい例として、同じく石を使ったロバート・スミッソンの《ノン・サイト》を考えてみよう。作家の作品を〈表現〉と〈オペレーション〉に分解した作戦は、ここでも有効に機能する。表現の国際的同時性は必ずしもオペレーションの国際的同時性を意味しないからだ。

美術史では一種のタブーでもある市場制度の考察が要素として浮上してくる。ニューヨークやパリのように商業画廊制度が機能しているのか、いないのか。その違いだけでも、作家の〈判断〉や行動は変わってくる。実際、GUNがグループ展を連続的に仕掛けることができたのは、賃料を払いさえすれば1週間展示スペースを確保できる貸画廊制度のおかげ

first year. However, from 1969 onward, their financial limitations forced them to explore the possibility of non-exhibition activities in their region. One major outcome was *Event to Change the Image of Snow*, with which they succeeded in nationwide media exposure. However, their main activities consisted of individual projects under the banner of GUN.

Generally speaking, a group structured as an exhibition society tends to collapse when unable to continue exhibitions. It would have been no surprise if GUN had disbanded in 1969. However, thanks to the one year of energetic exhibition activities, GUN achieved a certain level of recognition. Therefore, they managed to secure the existence of GUN as an operational platform by using the calling card of "Horikawa Michio of GUN" or "Maeyama Tadashi of GUN." Unusual as it may be as a form of collectivism, this was an ingenious strategy the young artists devised within a limited range of options they had in the wilderness.

Needless to say, securing an operational platform is one thing, making an advance in expression is quite another. Horikawa's *Mail Art by Sending Stones* was born in this struggle, inventively taking his expression out of the exhibition system.

Exhibition is a typical operational mode for artists in presenting their expressions and creating a circuit of communication in society. In 1960s Japan, as exemplified by Hi Red Center's so-called *Cleaning Event* of 1964, some practitioners took their expressions outside the exhibition, thereby merging "expression" (action/information) and "operation" (presentation and communication in society). The Play further advanced the merging of expression and operation, as they purposefully organized and disseminated the information after their expression. Moreover, they expanded the definition of membership to include collaborating non-members, thus anticipating a new direction of social engagement.

Mail art, too, takes expression out of the exhibition system. In the case of Horikawa, the object (stones) is his expression as much as the act (mailing stones) is, while the latter also constitutes his operation. Hence, expression and operations are merged in his mail art.

Furthermore, he actively created a second life for the act of mailing by compiling data cards. This gave an additional dimension of networking to his information operation.

The separation of expression and operation, which I initially introduced in my study of collectivism, is also effective in the study of conceptualism. If we rephrase the division as "what to express = information" and "how to operationally communicate = information-ization," operation can be visualized in a spectrum that ranges from exhibition to mailing, from direct presentation to information-ization. Here, Horikawa's stone mailing encompasses the whole spectrum, thanks to the duality of his project centering on both the object and the act.

Global: International Contemporaneity and Comparison

—

To study *Mail Art by Sending Stones* in the context of the wilderness is to study it in a localized context. It combines a micro (individual) study of expression and a local-macro (structural) study of operation. How, then, will this story be linked to a globalized art history?

A macro framework that encompasses a number of local histories of Japan as well as other non-Western and Western areas is "international contemporaneity" (*kokusaiteki dōjisei*) that emerged in the global 1960s. The term has been taken from the critics Miyakawa Atsushi and Haryū Ichirō, who discoursed on the sense of "international contemporaneity," which these Japanese critics could discern because of the long-held consciousness of "belatedness." The methodology to visualize this framework is comparative art history, for which in my case Japan serves as a paradigmatic site that helps us dismantle the established ideas, values, and logics in art history.

One strategy was to study "resonances" in "similar yet dissimilar" works, where no actual "connections" exist. Through comparing these works, we can identify and amplify multiple narrative tangents.

For example, let us compare Horikawa's *Mail Art by Sending Stones* and Robert Smithson's *Non-Site*, a

だった（こういう画廊の制度はニューヨークには存在していない）。一方、スミッソンの周辺には現代美術の商業画廊とコレクターが存在し、スミッソンのようなアースワークの作家も有形無形に支援を受けていた。堀川の石は、『美術手帖』で見たスミッソンが（商業）画廊制度の内外を対比させた《ノン・サイト》に微弱な繋がりがある。だがむしろ、直接的には画廊の内外を可視化した日本の作例、高松次郎の《石と数字》のインスピレーションが大きい（ちなみに、これも『美術手帖』からの学習効果だ）。しかも予算皆無の「悪い場所」からアポロ11号に触発されてイマジネーションを宇宙空間に飛翔させた逸物だった。スミッソンの石は最初から画廊の中に設置される売買可能なモノとして構想されていたのに対して、堀川の石は、市場の外側で、何が作品なのか、という根源的な問いを要請した。実際、この比較を考えると、市場の欠如は表現の自由を保障してすらいる。戦後日本はそんなに「悪い場所」だったのか、とあらためて問わざるを得ない。

　（なお、両者の詳細な比較は、英文による論考「石の上にいかに世界美術史を構築するか：堀川紀夫と同時代作家たちを位置付ける」を共著の論文集『トランスナショナルな視点から考える日本美術』に刊行予定）。

　さて〈似て非なるもの〉による比較美術史は、周縁から起動できる知識量拡充のための挑発的戦略でもある。「未知」を「周知」にぶつけることで、「未知」を「周知」に変えていくという戦略だ。〈響きあい〉の研究は、表現が〈似て非なる〉というその一点から出発して言説を作っていける。トランスナショナルな歴史の定石である〈繋がり〉研究の盲点を補うのが〈響きあい〉の比較なのだ。

　さらに、〈国際的同時性〉とは、西洋相対化（地方化）の視点を潜在させている。日本だけに限っても、具体のアクションや松澤宥のコンセプチュアリズムのように従来の欧米先行のナラティブにオルタナティブを示しうる事例はいくつもある。

　戦後美術や60年代美術における既成の歴史観を解体し、新たな歴史のナラティブを再構築していく──美術史家としてこれほどやりがいのある挑戦はない。

未知を周知にぶつけることで、周知も脱神話化され、新たな見方が引き出されうる。

　時空の共有が〈国際的同時性〉の出現で、より等価になったとすれば、比較はむしろ当然であり、さらには西洋も一つのローカル、より正確には多くのローカルの集合体であることを再確認する手段ともなる。すなわち、それぞれの地域でそれぞれの地域のコンテクストとロジックでそれぞれのモダニズムが並行し、全体としての近代が共生的に形成された、ことの確認である。

結論にかえて
─

　言うまでもなく、世界美術史には多視点的探求が要請されるから、比較の対象は欧米（＝中心）に限らない。アジアにも南米にもアフリカにも、日本と同じように周縁と呼ばれていた地域へと広げていかなければ、真にグローバルな比較にはならない。その一方で、個別の研究で得られた新たな知見の普及もなおざりにはできない。

　スミッソンと堀川の比較で〈周知〉と〈未知〉の比較だと形容したが、概して中心と周縁では、それぞれに関する知識量の不均衡が厳然と存在する。日本やアジアを専門としない研究者や美術館学芸員などへも知識が波及していかなければ、知識量の不均衡は解消しないだろう。知識の拡散は、学会の内部よりも、むしろ美術館での展示や普及教育、大学などの教養レベルで美術史の授業が行われる教室などで進んでいく。

　現状では、世界美術史を戦略的に考えて組まれた戦後あるいは60年代日本美術史の通史的教科書となりうるものは存在しない。経糸がしっかりしていないと、中心地域とであれ、他の周縁地域とであれ比較による輻輳を横糸としてしっかり編み込んでいけない。グローバルであるためには、ローカル（足元）から固めていく必要もある。

　では、その教科書とはどのような内容になるだろうか。まず、総花的に基準作品（benchmark）を並べるだけではつまらない。何よりも欧米モダニズムを専門と

contemporary series based on stones and other earth matter. The separation of expression and operation is effective here, too. That is because the international contemporaneity of expression does not always mean that of operation.

A taboo subject in art history, the market system has to be factored into this comparison. Was there any functional commercial system, like that in Paris or New York, in Japan? This difference certainly affected the artist's judgement and activities. In fact, the existence of the rental gallery system, especially in Tokyo, wherein anybody could have an exhibition for a week by paying the fees, made it possible for GUN to mount a series of group exhibitions for one year. (No similar system existed in New York.) Smithson, in contrast, was situated in the commercial market system and his large-scale land projects benefited from this system and willing collectors and supporters. Horikawa's use of stones has a weak connection to Smithson's *Non-Site*, a photograph of which the Japanese artist saw in the art magazine *Bijutsu techō*. But more importantly the young artist was inspired by Takamatsu Jirō's *Stone and Numeral* (also seen in *Bijutsu techō*), which explicitly contrasted the inside and outside of the gallery space. Furthermore, Horikawa flew his imagination into outer space from a "bad place" of no budget, in dialogue with the Apollo 11 mission. While Smithson's *Non-Site* was conceived as a commodity to be installed in the gallery space, Horikawa conceived his mailing outside the marketplace, while demanding us to ask the fundamental question: What is a work of art? In this particular comparison, we can see the lack of marketplace afforded an artist a great deal of freedom. If so, we must ask again: Was postwar Japan such a bad place?

(A full comparison is undertaken in my "How to Build a World Art History on Stones: Or, Siting Horikawa Michio and His Contemporaries," an essay to be published in a forthcoming anthology *Japanese Art: Transcultural Perspectives*.)

Comparative art history based on "similar yet dissimilar" works is a strategy to expand the amount of information on the periphery initiated by the periph-

ery. By comparing the "unknown" and the "known," we aim to transform "unknown" into "known." The study of resonances can be initiated with two works similar in expression with no connections whatsoever, enabling us to weave a new narrative. Resonance study fills the blind spot of connection study, a conventional methodology of transnational art history.

Most importantly, "international contemporaneity" encompasses a potential for relativization (or provincialization) of the West. In 1960s Japan alone, there are numerous examples, including Gutai's actions and Matsuzawa Yutaka's conceptualism, that point to the need for an alternative narrative to the ingrained Western-led story.

To deconstruct the established historical narrative of postwar and 1960s art and constitute a new narrative—what can be more rewarding a task for an art historian? By putting the known and unknown on the same stage, we will not only demystify the known but also possibly find a new view for the known.

If the sharing of time-space led to the equivalency that is characterized by international contemporaneity, comparison should logically follow. In doing so we can reconfirm that the West itself is another locale, or more precisely, a collection of many locales. In other words, we can reconfirm the multiplicity of modernisms that evolved in parallel and co-constitute modernity as a whole.

In Lieu of Conclusion

–

Needless to say, world art history demands exploration from multiple viewpoints. The object of comparison is not limited to those works of Euro-America (the center) and our study must be expanded to other peripheral areas, including Asia, Africa, and Latin America. Otherwise, our comparison will not be truly global. Having said that, it is also imperative to disseminate the knowledge and insight thus gained.

At the present moment, there undeniably exists inequity of knowledge about the center and that about the margins. That is a structural reason for comparison of the known and unknown, like Smithson's and

する研究者に「作家の判断がよく分かった」と思える
ような記述にしないことには、世界美術史の貢献とし
ての意義がないだろう。とすると、作品がよくなけれ
ば話にならないが、その上で選択には、いくつかの条
件が考えられる。

1. 作品が〈国際的同時性〉を体現している
2. 作品にいくつもの要素があり、それぞれがロー
   カルへの入り口になりナラティブ接線を形成する

　第一はさておき、第二の条件は、作品を表現の次元
のみならず、オペレーションの次元でも系統的に説明
するために必要な視点となる。こうして選んだ作品
は、〈国際的同時代性〉の基準作となるのみならず、比
較の基準作であり、さらには、60年代世界美術史全体
の基準作の候補でもある。
　堀川の《石を送るメール・アート》は基準作候補の
資格が十二分にあるだろう。石は一見普遍的なよう
で、様々な出自があり、それを検討するだけでローカ
ルな地勢的また地学的な検討材料になるとともに、石
そのものへの文化的社会的視線も様々だ。堀川の
シリーズでは、荒野のみならず、メール・アート、行為
の情報化の系譜など、ナラティブ接線は豊富だ。し
かも、スミッソンの《ノン・サイト》との比較では、
ローカルな状況をも反映して、鮮やかなコントラスト
をなし、〈国際的同時性〉の基準作としても強い印象
を残してくれるにちがいない。
　表現とオペレーションの二つの次元から、基準作と
なる作品を考察し、日本の60年代美術を今一度ふりか
える。それが私の次の大仕事になるだろう。

Horikawa's stones. Still, if the knowledge and insight did not spread among scholars and curators not specializing in Japan or Asia, the inequity would not be resolved. The dissemination of knowledge is needed not so much within the narrow confines of a specific area study as in the broader spheres of museums (through exhibitions and educations) and university classrooms (through especially undergraduate courses of art history and visual culture).

In this respect, there is no survey-style textbook of 1960s art in Japan written within a strategic framework of world art history. We need sturdy warps to weave a tapestry of world art history enlivened by comparative wefts among locales in the center and margins. Global picturing requires solid local components.

What, then, does such a textbook look like? It cannot be a mere list of benchmark works. In order for it to be a contribution to world art history, it must enunciate "the artist's judgments" that underpin these works. Selected works will have to meet these two requirements:

1. Each work must embody international contemporaneity.
2. Each work must contain multiple elements which form entry points to the local and generate relevant narrative tangents.

While the first is obvious, the second enables us to systematically examine the work in both expression and operation. These works will not only constitute the benchmark of international contemporaneity but also that of comparative studies, and ultimately of 1960s art in world art history.

Horikawa's *Mail Art by Sending Stones* is certainly a worthy candidate as a benchmark. Although stones are ordinary objects, they are in fact marked by their origins geographically and geologically. They are further a subject of socio-cultural studies. With Horikawa's stone mailing, several narrative tangents converge: the wilderness, mail art, an act and its information as *sakuhin*, to just name a few. Through the comparison with Smithson's *Non-Sites*, it amply demonstrates local situations and presents a vivid contrast.

To study "benchmark" works in terms of both expression and operation and survey 1960s art in Japan again. That will be my next big project.

(Translated from the Japanese original by the author)

おわりに

《石を送るメール・アート》は生成30年後に美術史家富井玲子の論考に取り上げられ、作品としての息を吹き返しました。私は、《石》を再開する論理を獲得するに至りました。《石》は生成時のコンセプトを纏って螺旋を描いて再生成を遂げ、機に応じて送り続けられてきました。

《石》は、自然石、針金、荷札（切手と消印を含む）の3つの要素でできています。巻かれた針金を外せば《石》は直ちに元の石に還ります。針金は錆び、荷札は劣化していきます。これまでに送付された《石》が今日の時点でどこにどうあるのかは、受け取られた人それぞれに属し、明らかではありません。その視点から宮沢壮佳や松沢宥が1969年の《石》を今日まで劣化を防いで大切に保管してこられたことを知り大感謝・感動でした。

《石》を送る、運ぶ、受け取るなどの手続きに直接関わられた皆様には剥き出しの石に荷札が付いた姿で驚かせ、ご迷惑をおかけしました。送付された皆様のお名前を覚書で敬称略にて公表させていただきました。その手前勝手さをお許しください。

《石》はNYでの展示後 Misa Shin Gallery 辛美沙のもとで新たな舞台に誘われ、内外の展示施設に収蔵されました。私は描いた夢以上のことが実現し、大いに喜び、そして恐縮しています。

今日の私は《石》を中心に据え、絵画、彫刻、オブジェ、パフォーマンス、メール・アート、Eメール・アート、E-Stamps、Tensegrity（テンセグリティ）による立体表現、CGオートマティズムなど様々な表現を随意応変に展開しています。76歳を過ぎ、アートに関わって思いのままに創作、発表、享受を楽しむ日々を過ごし、とても幸せな心境にいます。

さて、宇宙開発は平和目的から宇宙軍創設に及んでスパイ、ミサイル監視の衛星技術を競い合い、一方で大富豪が巨額の代価を払って10分程度の宇宙旅行を自慢し合う時代となっています。これを人類の進歩と言えるでしょうか。

また、ロシアによるウクライナ侵攻が2月24日に始まりました。ハイテク兵器による爆撃、殺戮、破壊が現在進行中。その戦争現場のおぞましい画像や動画に恐怖を感じています。早期停戦も見通せず、国際社会が急激に不安定化しています。

アートは平和と愛の言葉を創造・享受することです。人間としてアーティストとしてこの戦争にどう対峙し行動・表現していくか問われています。私は「地球の石」をコンセプトに《石》を継続してきました。今後とも、この《石》により、平和と愛、人類進歩につながる意味を追求し続けます。

本書は私の初めての作品集です。富井玲子のバイリンガルによる3つの論文をいただいて本書を世に出すことができ、《石》をグローバルに刻印することができたと考えています。本書をこれまで私を支えてくれた家族、友人、知人、関係者全ての皆様に捧げます。出版にあたり、現代企画室にお世話いただきました。心より感謝申しあげます。

堀川紀夫 (2022.5)

Mail Art by Sending Stones was revived as a work of art 30 years after its birth through the art historian Reiko Tomii's study, which prompted me to articulate the principle of resuming the *Stones* series. *Stones* thus gained a renewed life, with the initial concept reiterated. I have since sent stones when I found fitting occasions.

Each *Stone* consists of three elements: a natural stone, wires, and mailing tags (stamped and postmarked). When the wires are removed, *Stones* return to their original natural state. The wires rust and the mailing tags deteriorate. The present whereabouts of the *Stones* I sent in the past are not always known, with their treatment varying from recipient to recipient. In this regard, I am more than grateful that some recipients, including Miyazawa Takeyoshi and Matsuzawa Yutaka, have preserved the first *Stones* of 1969 in good condition.

I would like to apologize to those who were directly involved with *Stones* as they were sent, carried, and received for all the trouble and surprises I caused them. In this book, I have made public the names of the recipients. I hope you will forgive my selfish act.

After exhibited in New York, *Stones* went onto a new stage at Misa Shin Gallery, from which they now have been collected in a few museums in Japan and abroad. These developments are more than I dreamed of a long time ago. I am at once pleased and humbled.

Today, centering on the *Stones* series, my activities take a range of forms: painting, sculpture, *objets*, performance, mail art, e-mail art, E-Stamps, Tensegrity objects, and CG-automatism. Having passed 76, I feel very happy every day, making, presenting, and enjoying art to my heart's content.

In our lifetime, space exploration has expanded from peaceful applications to the idea of space forces, with the competition for new technologies heating up in the area of satellite surveillance and missile launch-es. At the same time, some billionaires who dominate global economy compete to make a ten-minute travel into outer space by spending an unfathomable sum of money. I wonder if this means humankind has made progress.

On February 24, 2022, Russia began the invasion of Ukraine. As of this writing, Russia's bombing, killing, and destruction have continued with the deployment of hi-tech weapons. The horrifying photographs and videos from the war zones send a shudder through our spine. With little prospect for early resolution, the international world is rapidly destabilizing.

Through art, we create and cherish the language of peace and love. This war has raised a question to me: how to face this reality and take action as a human being and make art as an artist.

I have continued my *Mail Art by Sending Stones* with the basic concept of "earth stone." With this series, I will continue to explore its meaning in peace, love, and progress of humankind.

This is the first monographic book on my work. With this book, three bilingual essays by Reiko Tomii are sent into the world to make a global mark with *Stones*. This book is dedicated to all those who have supported me: my family, friends and acquaintances, and other people involved in my art. I sincerely thank Gendaikikakushitsu for publishing this book under their imprint.

Horikawa Michio (2022.5)

「石の上にも三年」という言葉がある。思えば、堀川紀夫の《石を送るメール・アート》と付き合いはじめてほぼ四半世紀になる。シリーズの存在を知ったのが1995年頃、ニューヨークのクイーンズ美術館が企画したグローバル・コンセプチュアリズム展（1999年開催）の日本セクション・キュレーターとして調査をしていた時だった。そして、同展の出品作家だった彦坂尚嘉から教えられて、新潟に作家を訪れ作品調査を行い、ロンドンのテート・モダンの開館記念特別展「センチュリー・シティ」（2001年開催）に出品していただいた。さらにはニューヨークのジャパン・ソサエティでの荒野のラジカリズム：グローバル60年代の日本の現代美術家たち展（2019年）でも大きく取り上げることができた。

個別の作品論は、日本語では本書再録の論考1（2010年）と論考2（2019年）で一定の成果を上げたと自負している。また、英語では荒野のラジカリズム展の出発点となった2016年上梓の『Radicalism in the Wilderness: International Contemporaneity and 1960s Art in Japan』で詳述していた。

新たに書きおろした論考3では、個別の作家論や作品論を越えて、歴史化の課題と戦略を考えた。ここで言う「歴史化」とは、世界美術史に戦後日本美術を定着させていく作業のことであり、そのためには戦略的思考が要請される。その思考を構築する中で、私にとって《石を送るメール・アート》は、堀川が前山忠と主導したグループGUNの《雪のイメージを変えるイベント》や《郵送戦線》などの仕事とあわせて、決定的な役割を果たした。

* * *

美術史家の仕事は、作家が作品を作ったところから始まる。私の《石を送るメール・アート》への興味は「面白い作品だ」という人並みの感想から始まった。世界美術史などという大仕事になるとは思わないで

調査や研究を始めた。それは堀川の作品に限らないのだが、堀川の《石》は吸引力が強いだけではなく、表現の本質がオープンで、いくつもの思考のベクトルを発生させる。それを読めば読むほどに、作品が豊かになっていく。それを追いかけつつ私の研究も豊かになっていったと感じている。

と同時に、本書の編集作業を通じて改めて学ぶことも少なくなかった。特に、掲載用写真を整理しながら、半世紀にわたる《石》そのものの表情に見入るとともに、それらに付された荷札に変化のあることにも気付かされた。「地球の石＝ the stone on the earth」の経緯については、作家も「覚書」で語っているが、他にも「MAIL ART」の印が押されている荷札もあれば、「反戦＝ anti-War」を印刷した荷札もある。

個人的には2000年12月8日に発送された《石》を受け取った時に「JAPS BOMB HAWAII」の荷札が目に飛び込んできてギョッとした。これは私の地元ニューヨークの『デイリー・ニュース』紙の一面特大見出しを借用したもので、真珠湾攻撃にちなんだメール・アートになっていた。「意味が見つかれば《石》の再開はあり得る」と言っていた作家の言葉に意味のあったことを即座に理解したが、その荷札がいくつか他の《石》にも使われているのを今回知って感慨深かった。

　たかが石、されど石
　石の上に四半世紀
　石の上に世界美術史

富井玲子

There is a Japanese saying, "Even a stone may feel warm, if one sits on it for three years." I have studied Horikawa Michio's *Mail Art by Sending Stones* for almost a quarter century. I first came to know about it around 1995 during my research for the Japanese section of *Global Conceptualism* (opened in 1999 at Queens Museum of Art in New York). Hikosaka Naoyoshi, one of the artists I was considering for my section, told me about Horikawa's stone project. When I was asked to curate the Tokyo section for *Century City* (opened in 2001 at Tate Modern in London), I included Horikawa's mail art. In 2019, when I curated *Radicalism in the Wilderness: Japanese Artists in the Global 1960s* (opened in 2019 at Japan Society in New York), his mail art occupied an important place.

Since the first presentation at Tate Modern, I have refined my study of the project, as shown in Text 1 (2010) and Text 2 (2019), both originally written in Japanese and included bilingually in this volume. In English, I extensively discussed *Mail Art by Sending Stones* in *Radicalism in the Wilderness: International Contemporaneity and 1960s Art in Japan* (MIT Press, 2016), which served as the basis of the Japan Society exhibition (2019).

In Text 3, newly written for this book, I went beyond monographic studies and considered the challenge and strategy for historicization. What I mean by "historicization" is situating postwar Japanese art in world art history, a task that demands strategic thinking. In the process of devising such a strategy, *Mail Art by Sending Stones* by Horikawa and *Event to Change the Image of Snow* by GUN, a collective led by Horikawa and his fellow artist Maeyama Tadashi, have played a crucial role.

* * *

The work of an art historian begins where the artist makes a work. My initial interest in *Mail Art by Sending Stones* began with a simple fascination, a rather ordinary observation that it's interesting. I never expected that my examination of it would evolve into a foundational study for world art history. Horikawa's stone mailing is not only evocative; it is open as an expression directing us to various critical investigations. The more we read it, the richer it becomes. As I have followed its leads, my work, too, has become richer.

At the same time, while editing this book, I was still learning more than a few new things. Especially when I reviewed the photographs for illustration, I was struck by the diverse appearances of *Stones*, as much as those of the mail tags attached to them. The artist himself explains the origin of the printed "the stone of the earth" mail tag, but some mail tags are stamped with the phrase "MAIL ART," and some are printed "anti-War."

Personally, I was much alarmed when I received a *Stone* he sent me on December 8, 2000 (the day of Pearl Harbor in Japanese time). One mail tag loudly announced: JAPS BOMB HAWAII. It was the famous heading that almost filled the entire first page of New York's *Daily News* on the day after the attack. He appropriated the page for his mail tag, signaling the fact that he had found the meaning to resume the series. I now understand he used the same mail tag in some of his subsequent *Stones*, which are reproduced in this volume.

It's just a stone, yet it's a stone.
A quarter century on Horikawa's stones.
A world art history envisioned on these stones.

Reiko Tomii

編著者紹介

–

堀川紀夫

–

美術家。1946年新潟県上越市清里区生まれ。1967年新潟現代美術家集団GUN結成に参加。1968年新潟大学教育学部卒、1986年上越教育大学大学院修了。

富井玲子

–

美術史家。1988年テキサス大学オースティン校美術史学科博士課程修了。以後ニューヨーク在住、国際現代美術センター（CICA）の上級研究員を経て1992年より無所属、世界美術史における日本の1960年代美術を中心に研究。「ポンジャ現懇」（ponja-genkon.net）を2003年に設立、主宰。英文単著『荒野のラジカリズム —— 国際的同時性と日本の1960年代美術』（MIT大学出版局、2016年）がロバート・マザーウェル出版賞を受賞、同書をもとに「荒野のラジカリズム —— グローバル1960年代の日本のアーティスト」展をジャパン・ソサエティ（ニューヨーク）で企画（2019年）。令和2年度文化庁長官表彰（文化発信・国際交流—日本美術研究）を受賞。

About the Authors

–

Horikawa Michio is an artist born in Jōetsu city, Niigata prefecture, Japan in 1946. He co-founded GUN: Niigata Contemporary Artists Collective in 1967. He received a B.A. from Niigata University in 1968 and an M.A. from Jōetsu University of Education in 1986.

Reiko Tomii received a Ph.D. in art history from the University of Texas at Austin in 1988. After serving as Senior Research Associate at CICA (Center for International Contemporary Arts) in New York, she has been active as an independent art historian and curator focusing on post-1945 Japanese art in the context of world art history of modernisms. She is co-director of PoNJA-Gen-Kon (est. 2003), a listserv group of specialists interested in contemporary Japanese art. Her recent publication is *Radicalism in the Wilderness: International Contemporaneity and 1960s Art in Japan* (MIT Press, 2016) received the 2017 Robert Motherwell Book Award. In 2019, based on the book, she curated *Radicalism in the Wilderness: Japanese Artists in the Global 1960s* at Japan Society Gallery in New York. In 2020, she received the Commissioner for Cultural Affairs Award from the Japanese government for cultural transmission and international exchange through postwar Japanese art history.

石を送るメール・アート読本
Mail Art by Sending Stones: A Reader

堀川紀夫 + 富井玲子 編著
Edited by Michio Horikawa + Reiko Tomii

和訳 + 英訳：富井玲子
English and Japanese translation: Reiko Tomii

英語編集：キャスリーン・M・フリエロ
Copyediting in English: Kathleen M. Friello

編集支援：MISA SHIN GALLERY（辛美沙 + 嘉悦貴之）
Editorial Support: MISA SHIN GALLERY (Misa Shin and Takayuki Kaetsu)

制作：現代企画室（小倉裕介）
Book Production: Gendaikikakushitsu Publishers (Yusuke Ogura)

装丁デザイン：星野哲也
Book Design: Tetsuya Hoshino

印刷：三永印刷株式会社
Printing: Sanei Printery Co., Ltd.

発行者：堀川紀夫
Publisher: Michio Horikawa

発行日：2022.10.31
Publication Date: October 31, 2022

発売所：株式会社現代企画室
〒150-0033 東京都渋谷区猿楽町29-18　ヒルサイドテラスA8
Contact: Gendaikikakushitsu Publishers Co., Ltd.
A8 Hillside Terrace, 29-18 Sarugaku-cho, Shibuya-ku, Tokyo 1500033 Japan
Tel: (+81) 3-3461-5082　Fax: (+81) 3-3461-5083
Mail: gendai@jca.apc.org

ISBN978-4-7738-2211-3 C0070 Y2800E
Printed in Japan